Origami Gone Wild

More than 20 Original Animal Designs

Other books by John Montroll:

Origami and Math Simple to Complex

Dinosaur Origami

Mythological Creatures and the Chinese Zodiac Origami

Origami Worldwide

Origami Under the Sea by John Montroll and Robert J. Lang

Sea Creatures in Origami by John Montroll and Robert J. Lang

Teach Yourself Origami Second Revised Edition

Bringing Origami to Life

Dollar Bill Animals in Origami

Bugs and Birds in Origami

Dollar Bill Origami

Classic Polyhedra Origami

A Constellation of Origami Polyhedra

Christmas Origami

Storytime Origami

Animal Origami for the Enthusiast

Origami for the Enthusiast

Super Simple Origami

Easy Origami

Birds in Origami

Favorite Animals in Origami

Easy Christmas Origami

Easy Dollar Bill Origami

Origami Gone Wild

More than 20 Original Animal Designs

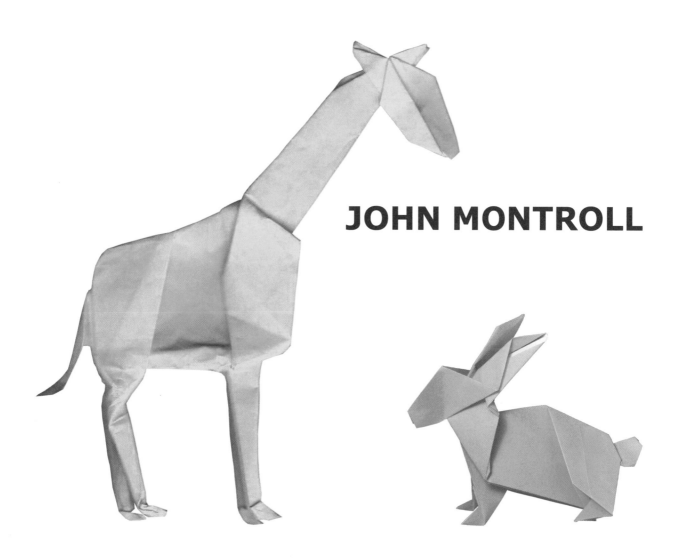

JOHN MONTROLL

Dover Publications, Inc.
New York

To Sarah and Elliott

Bibliographical Note

Origami Gone Wild: More Than 20 Original Animal Designs is a
new work, first published by Dover Publications, Inc., in 2012.

Library of Congress Cataloging-in-Publication Data

Montroll, John.
    Origami gone wild : more than 20 original animal
designs / John Montroll.
        p. cm.
    Summary: "From the internationally renowned origami master
comes this wild collection of more than 20 jungle and forest animals.
Models include an aardvark, panda, giraffe, rhinoceros, moose, and
zebra, ranging in complexity from fairly easy to advanced. This
guide's handsome, full-color format will appeal to a wide range of
paperfolders"—Provided by publisher.
    Summary: "Instructions for folding origami wild animals"—
Provided by publisher.
    ISBN-13: 978-0-486-49816-4 (pbk.)
    ISBN-10: 0-486-49816-6 (pbk.)
    1. Origami. 2. Wildlife art. I. Title.
TT870.M563   2012
736'.982–dc23   2012014201

Manufactured in the United States by Cenveo Publisher Services-Lancaster, PA Division
49816601
www.doverpublications.com

Introduction

Wild animals are among the most intriguing models to create, and to fold. With this collection of 25 models of varying degrees of complexity, you can make a baboon, elephant, giraffe, zebra, and many more. All the models follow my standard of using one square sheet with no cutting. Throughout this work you can explore new bases and structures.

The animals are arranged in alphabetical order from aardvark to zebra. Attention is given to detail, such as the hippopotamus's head, white tusks for the elephant, the facial expression of the baboon, and the stripes for the zebra. Models range from simple to very difficult. Two crocodiles are shown with different levels of complexity.

The original concept for this book was to simplify the organization of other books, and combine like-themed models from *African Animals in Origami*, *North American Animals in Origami*, and others. As I worked on this volume, I revised some of them and half are previously unpublished designs.

The diagrams are drawn in the internationally approved Randlett-Yoshizawa style, which is easy to follow once you have learned the basic folds. You can use any kind of square paper for these models, but the best results can be achieved using standard origami paper, which is colored on one side and white on the other. In these diagrams, the shading represents the colored side. Large sheets are easier to use than small ones. Origami supplies can be found in arts and craft shops, or visit Dover Publications online at www.doverpublications.com, or OrigamiUSA at www.origamiusa.org. You can find local and national groups practicing the art of origami around the world with online sites like OrigamiUSA's.

Printing in full color allows for more interesting content. I thank Himanshu Agrawal for his help in this project. I would like to thank my editor, Jan Polish. Thanks, also, to Charley Montroll for his help.

John Montroll

www.johnmontroll.com

Contents

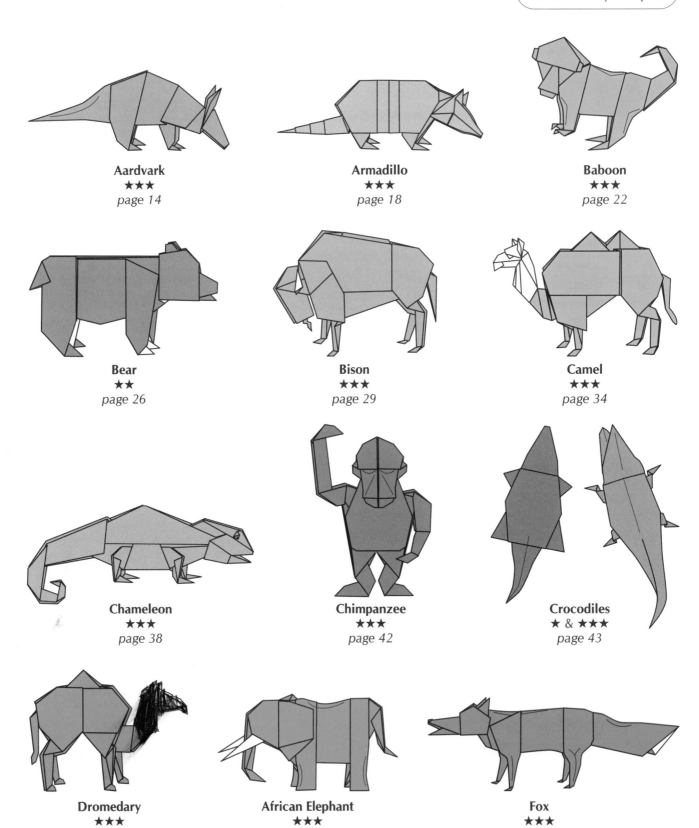

Symbols

Lines

— — — — — — — — — Valley fold, fold in front.

—·—··—··—··—··— Mountain fold, fold behind.

_____ Crease line.

.... X-ray or guide line.

Arrows

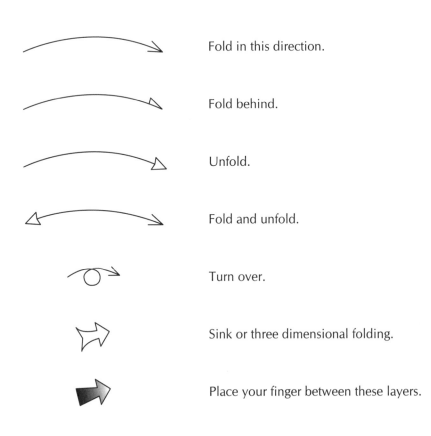

Fold in this direction.

Fold behind.

Unfold.

Fold and unfold.

Turn over.

Sink or three dimensional folding.

Place your finger between these layers.

Basic Folds

Pleat Fold.

Fold back and forth. Each pleat is composed of one valley and mountain fold. Here are two examples.

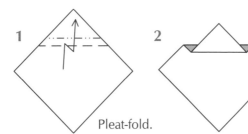

1   **2**

Pleat-fold.

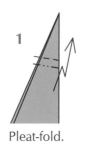 

1   **2**

Pleat-fold.

Squash Fold.

In a squash fold, some paper is opened and then made flat. The shaded arrow shows where to place your finger.

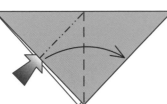 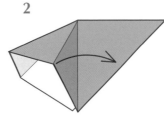 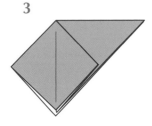

1   **2**   **3**

Squash-fold.   A 3D step.

Petal Fold.

In a petal fold, one point is folded up while two opposite sides meet each other.

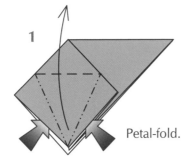 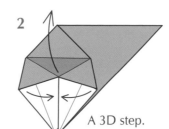 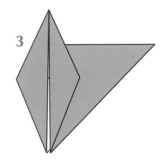

1   **2**   **3**

Petal-fold.   A 3D step.

Rabbit Ear.

To fold a rabbit ear, one corner is folded in half and laid down to a side.

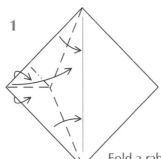 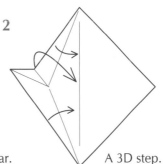 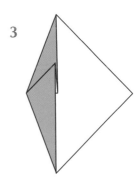

1   **2**   **3**

Fold a rabbit ear.   A 3D step.

Double Rabbit Ear.

If you were to bend a straw you would be folding the double rabbit ear.

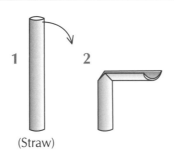 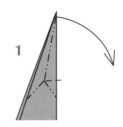 

1   **2**   **1**   **2**

(Straw)   Double-rabbit-ear.

Inside Reverse Fold.

In an inside reverse fold, some paper is folded between layers. Here are two examples.

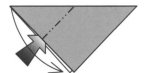 

Reverse-fold.

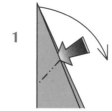 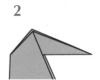

Reverse-fold.

Outside Reverse Fold.

Much of the paper must be unfolded to make an outside reverse fold.

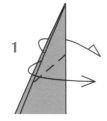 

Outside-reverse-fold.

Crimp Fold.

A crimp fold is a combination of two reverse folds. Open the model slightly to form the crimp evenly on each side. Here are two examples.

 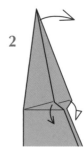 

Crimp-fold.   Crimp-fold.   A 3D step.

Sink.

For a sink, some of the paper without edges is folded inside. To do this fold, much of the model must be unfolded.

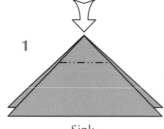 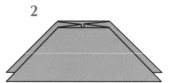

Sink.

Spread Squash Fold.

A cross between a squash fold and sink fold, some paper in the center is spread apart and then made flat.

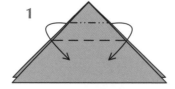 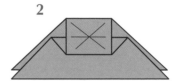

Spread-squash-fold.

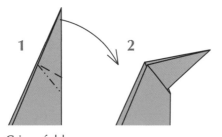

Preliminary Fold.

The Preliminary Fold is the starting point for many models. The maneuver in step 3 occurs often.

1

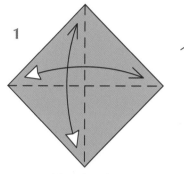

Fold and unfold.

2

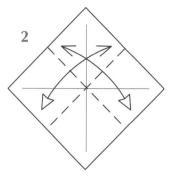

Fold and unfold.

3

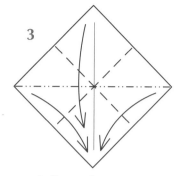

Collapse the square by bringing the four corners together.

4

This is 3D.

5

Preliminary Fold

Bird Base.

Historically, the Bird Base has been a very popular starting point. The folds used in it occur in many models.

1

Begin with the Preliminary Fold. Kite-fold, repeat behind.

2

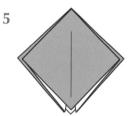

Unfold, repeat behind.

3

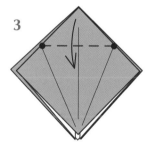

4

Unfold.

5

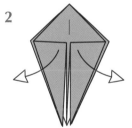

Petal-fold, repeat behind.

6

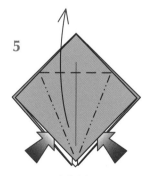

Repeat behind.

7

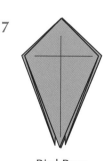

Bird Base

Blintz Frog Base.

This uses the double unwrap fold which is shown in detail below.

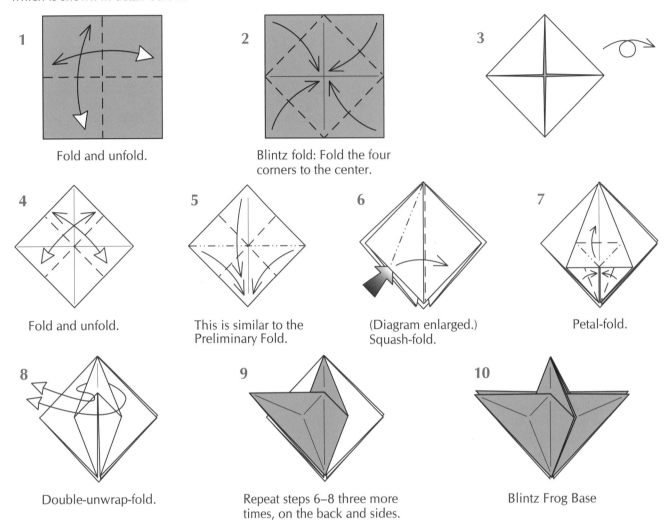

1

Fold and unfold.

2

Blintz fold: Fold the four corners to the center.

3

4

Fold and unfold.

5

This is similar to the Preliminary Fold.

6

(Diagram enlarged.) Squash-fold.

7

Petal-fold.

8

Double-unwrap-fold.

9

Repeat steps 6–8 three more times, on the back and sides.

10

Blintz Frog Base

Double Unwrap Fold.

In the double unwrap fold, locked layers are unwrapped and refolded. Much of the folding is 3D. The diagrams are depicted as shown in steps 8 and 9 of the Blintz Frog Base.

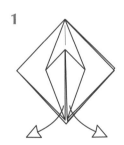

1

Begin with step 8 of the Blintz Frog Base. Spread at the bottom.

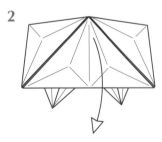

2

Unfold the top layer.

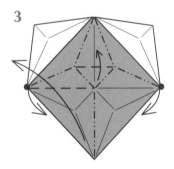

3

Refold along the creases. The dots will meet at the bottom.

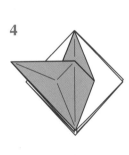

4

Origami Gone Wild

Aardvark

1

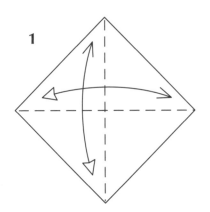

Fold and unfold.

2

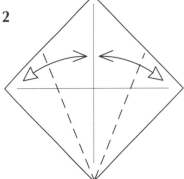

Kite-fold and unfold.

3

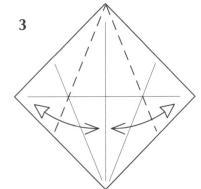

Kite-fold and unfold.

4

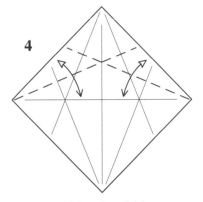

Fold and unfold.

5

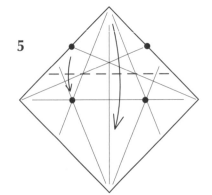

The dots will meet.

6

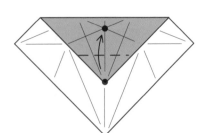

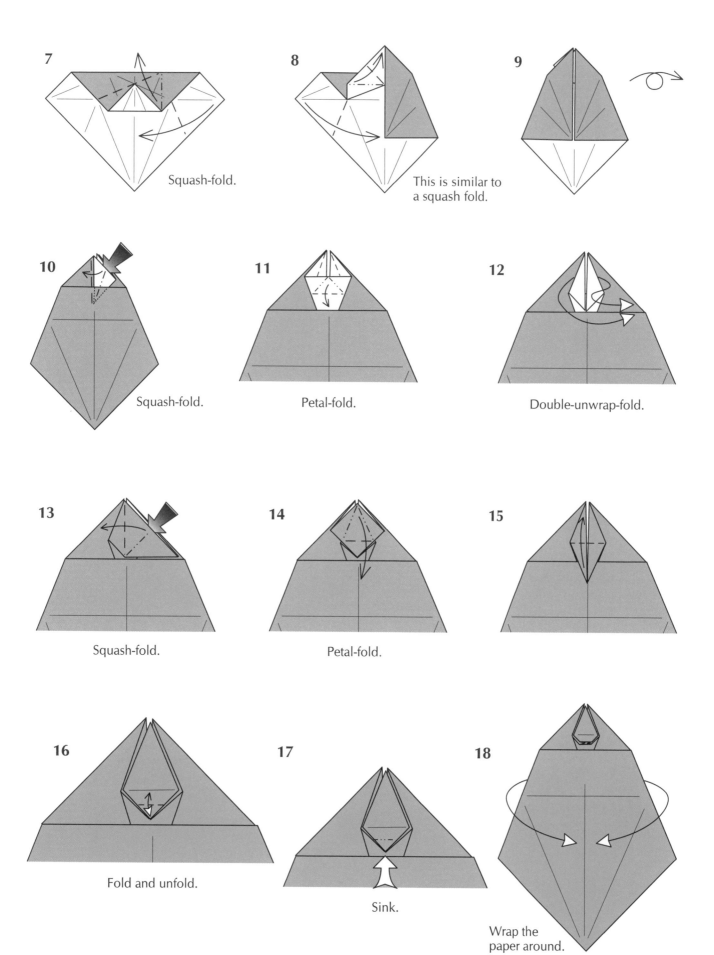

7 Squash-fold.

8 This is similar to a squash fold.

9

10 Squash-fold.

11 Petal-fold.

12 Double-unwrap-fold.

13 Squash-fold.

14 Petal-fold.

15

16 Fold and unfold.

17 Sink.

18 Wrap the paper around.

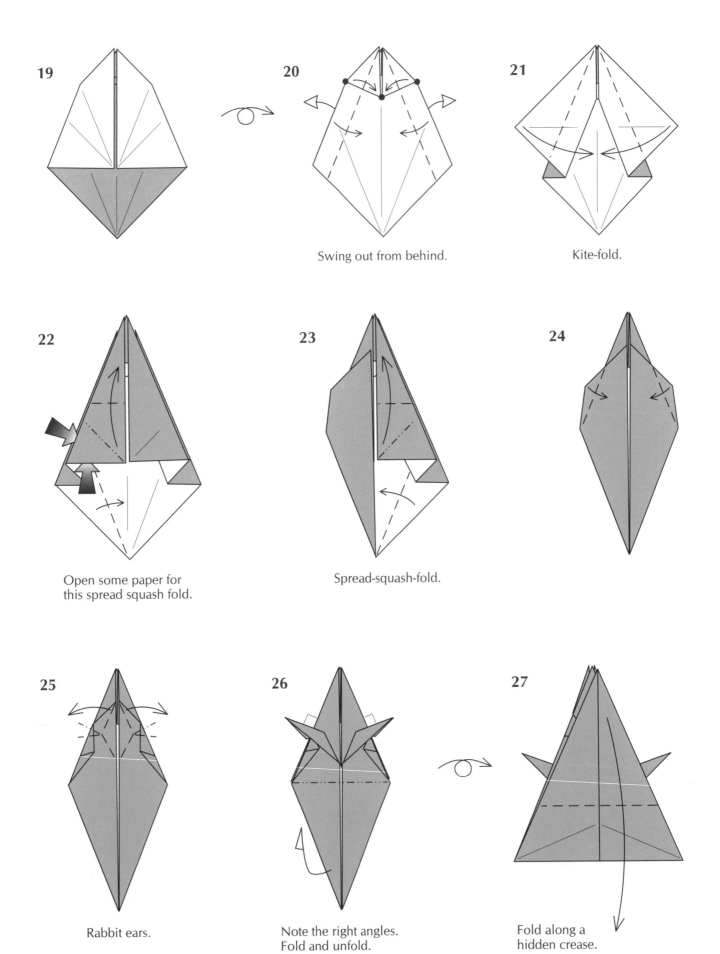

19

20

Swing out from behind.

21

Kite-fold.

22

Open some paper for
this spread squash fold.

23

Spread-squash-fold.

24

25

Rabbit ears.

26

Note the right angles.
Fold and unfold.

27

Fold along a
hidden crease.

28

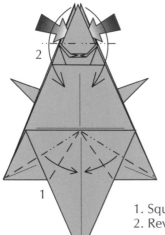

1. Squash folds.
2. Reverse folds.

29

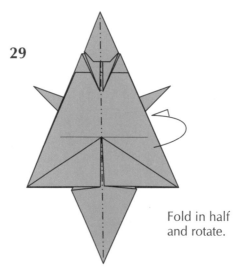

Fold in half
and rotate.

30

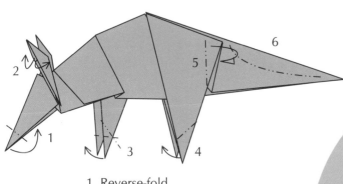

1. Crimp-fold.
2. Slide the head.

31

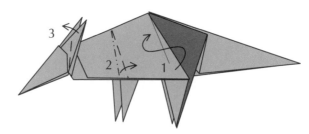

1. Tuck inside the dark paper.
2. Crimp-fold.
3. Valley-fold the ears.
Repeat behind.

32

1. Reverse-fold.
2. Open the ears.
3. Crimp-fold.
4. Reverse-fold.
5. Fold behind.
6. Shape the tail.
Repeat behind.

33

Aardvark

Armadillo

1

Fold and unfold.

2

Fold to the center.

3

Kite-fold.

4

5

Unfold everything.

6

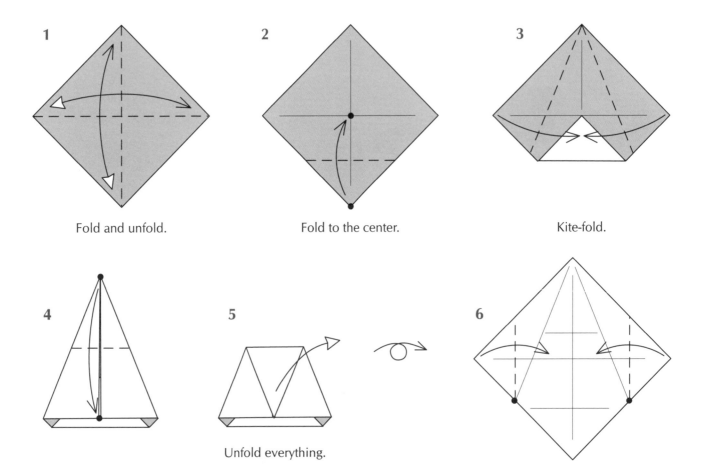

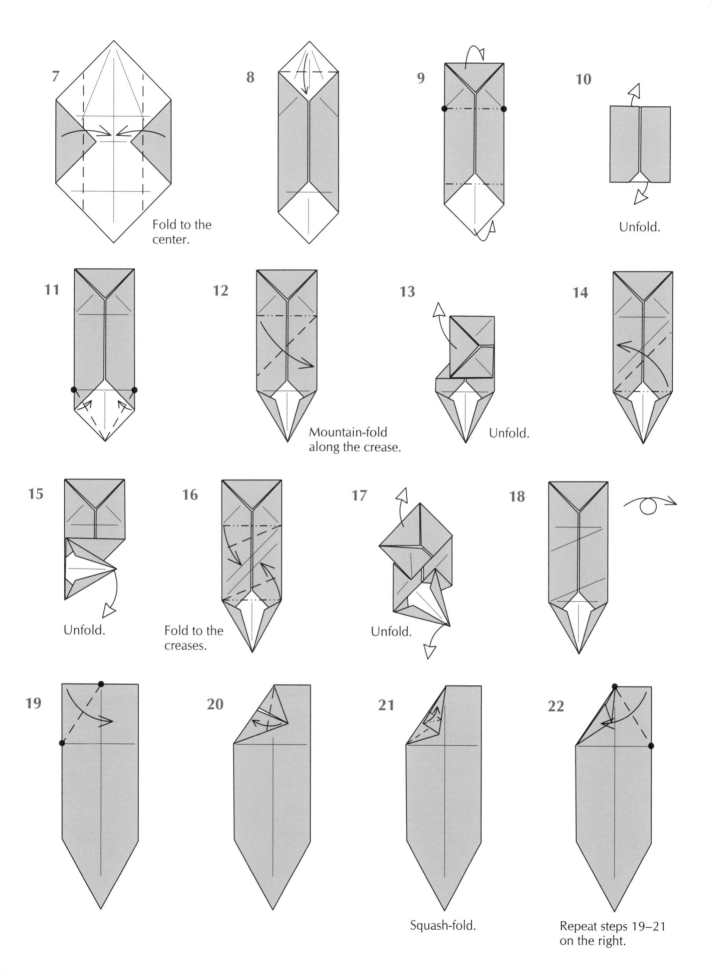

7 Fold to the center.

8

9

10 Unfold.

11

12 Mountain-fold along the crease.

13 Unfold.

14

15 Unfold.

16 Fold to the creases.

17 Unfold.

18

19

20

21 Squash-fold.

22 Repeat steps 19–21 on the right.

Armadillo 19

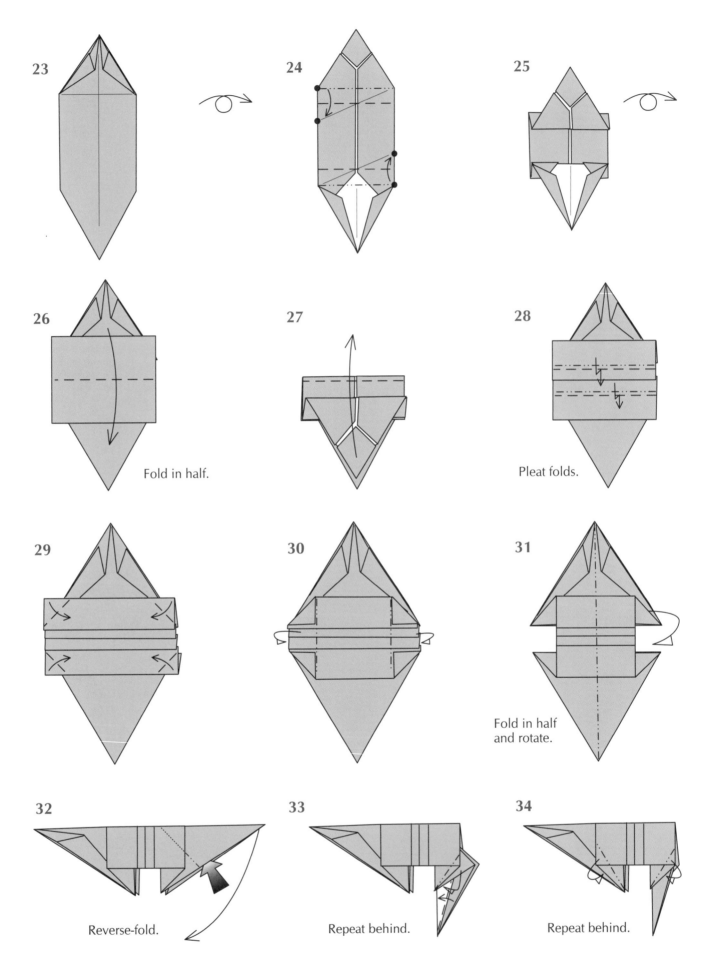

23

24

25

26

Fold in half.

27

28

Pleat folds.

29

30

31

Fold in half
and rotate.

32

Reverse-fold.

33

Repeat behind.

34

Repeat behind.

35

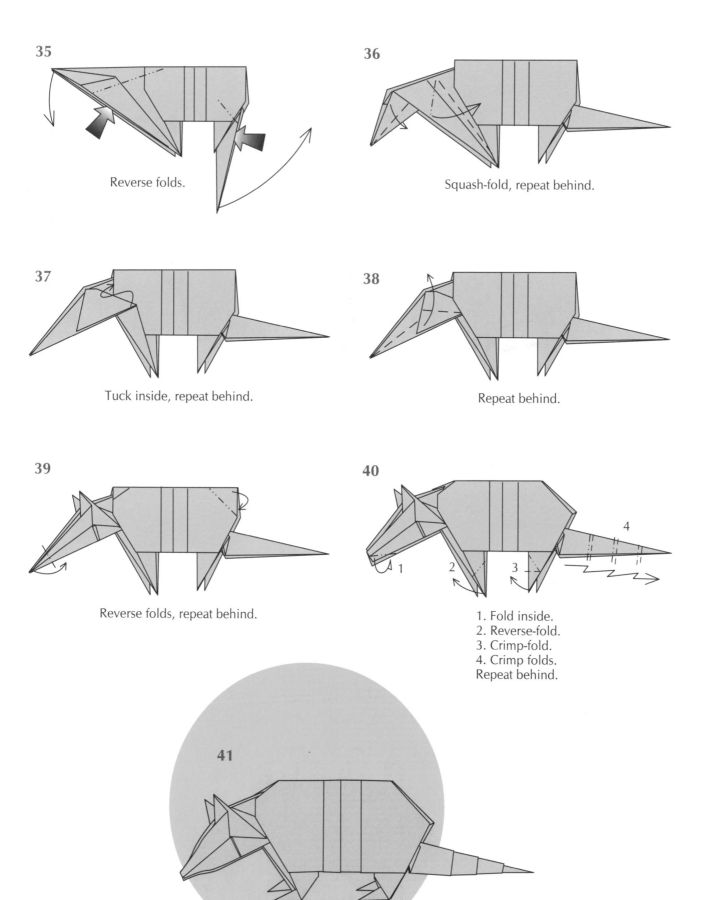

Reverse folds.

36

Squash-fold, repeat behind.

37

Tuck inside, repeat behind.

38

Repeat behind.

39

Reverse folds, repeat behind.

40

1. Fold inside.
2. Reverse-fold.
3. Crimp-fold.
4. Crimp folds.
Repeat behind.

41

Armadillo

Baboon

1

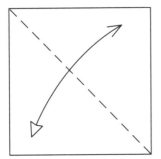

Fold and unfold.

2

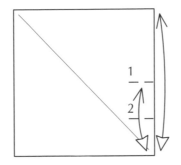

Fold and unfold
twice on the right to
find the 1/4 mark.

3

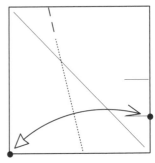

Bring the lower left corner
to the dot on the right. Fold
and unfold on the top.

4

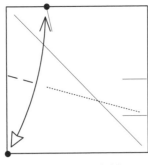

Fold and unfold
on the left.

5

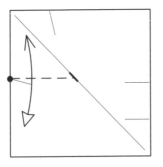

Fold and unfold
to the diagonal.

6

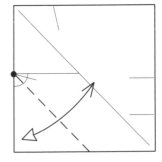

Fold and unfold.

7

Fold and unfold to the diagonal. Rotate.

8

Kite-fold and unfold.

9

Kite-fold and unfold.

10

Fold and unfold.

11

12

13

Make reverse folds along the creases.

14

Fold along the creases. Repeat behind.

15

Fold and unfold. Repeat behind.

16

Fold and unfold.

17

Fold the top layers along several of the creases.

18

Repeat steps 16–17 behind.

19

Petal-fold. Repeat behind.

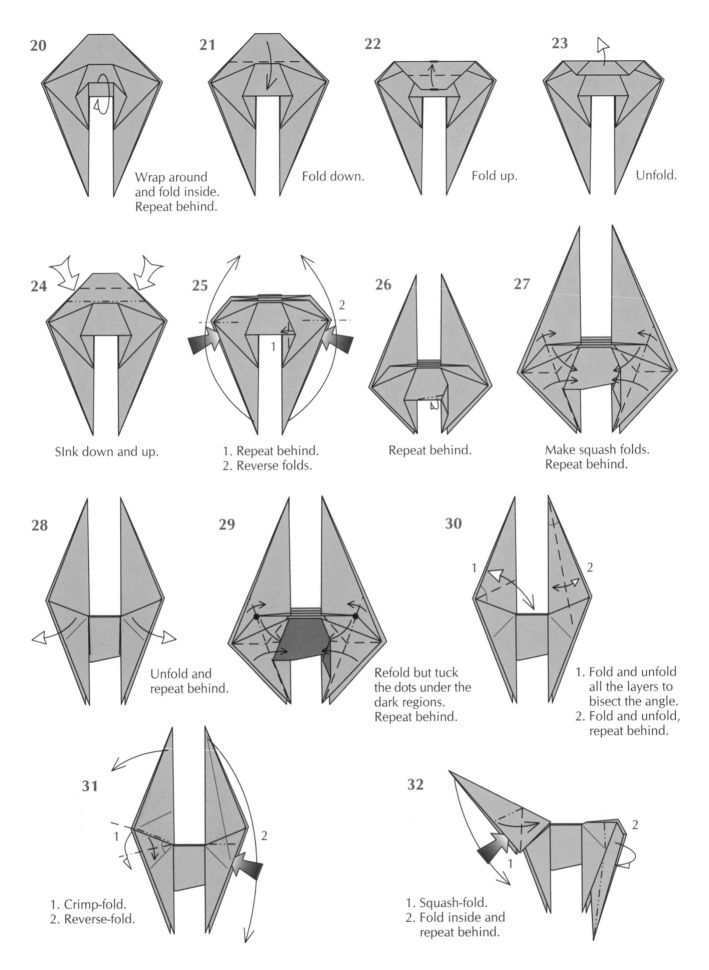

20 Wrap around and fold inside. Repeat behind.

21 Fold down.

22 Fold up.

23 Unfold.

24 Sink down and up.

25
1. Repeat behind.
2. Reverse folds.

26 Repeat behind.

27 Make squash folds. Repeat behind.

28 Unfold and repeat behind.

29 Refold but tuck the dots under the dark regions. Repeat behind.

30
1. Fold and unfold all the layers to bisect the angle.
2. Fold and unfold, repeat behind.

31
1. Crimp-fold.
2. Reverse-fold.

32
1. Squash-fold.
2. Fold inside and repeat behind.

33

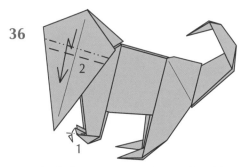

Reverse-fold.

34

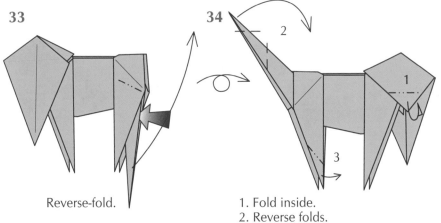

1. Fold inside.
2. Reverse folds.
3. Reverse-fold and repeat behind.

35

1. Fold behind.
2. Outside-reverse-fold but slightly twisted. Repeat behind.

36

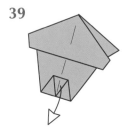

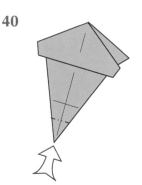

The baboon can stand on its hind legs.
1. Repeat behind.
2. Pleat-fold.

37

Only the head is drawn.

38

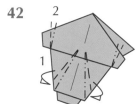

39

Unfold.

40

Sink (or reverse-fold).

41

Mountain-fold along the crease for this pleat fold.

42

Pleat folds.

43

Shape the back and legs.

44

Baboon

Bear

1

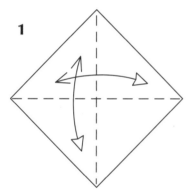

Fold and unfold.

2

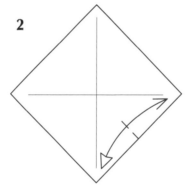

Fold and unfold
on the edge.

3

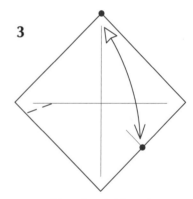

Fold and unfold on the
left so the dots meet.

4

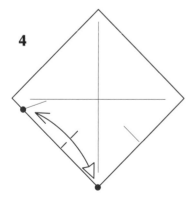

Fold and unfold on the
left so the dots meet.

5

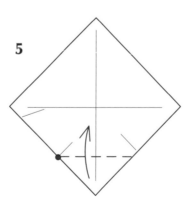

6

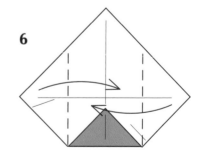

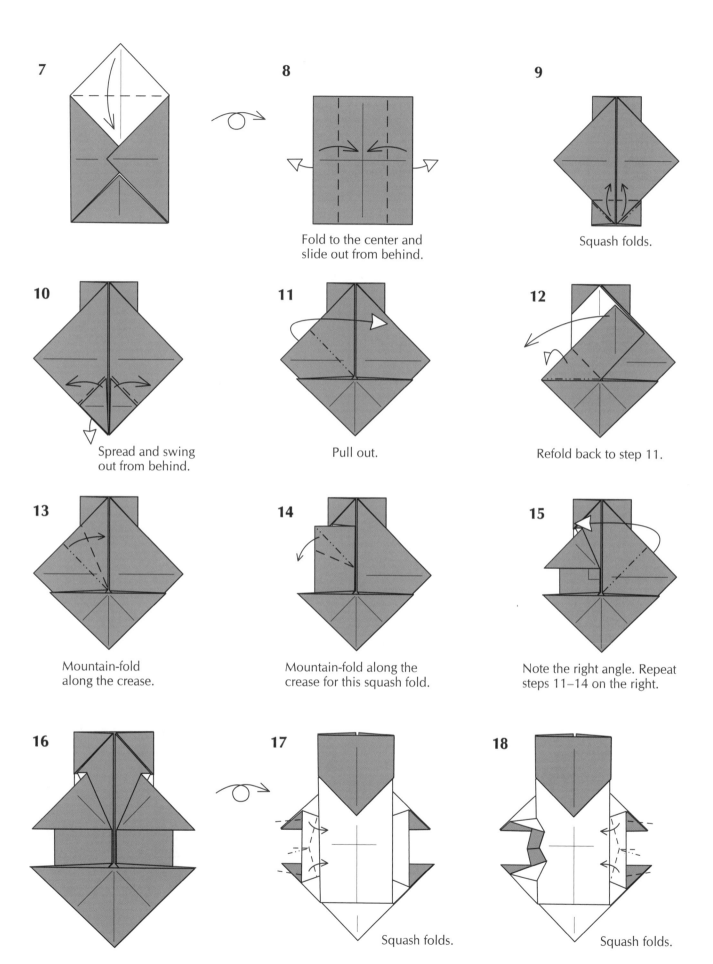

7

8

Fold to the center and
slide out from behind.

9

Squash folds.

10

Spread and swing
out from behind.

11

Pull out.

12

Refold back to step 11.

13

Mountain-fold
along the crease.

14

Mountain-fold along the
crease for this squash fold.

15

Note the right angle. Repeat
steps 11–14 on the right.

16

17

Squash folds.

18

Squash folds.

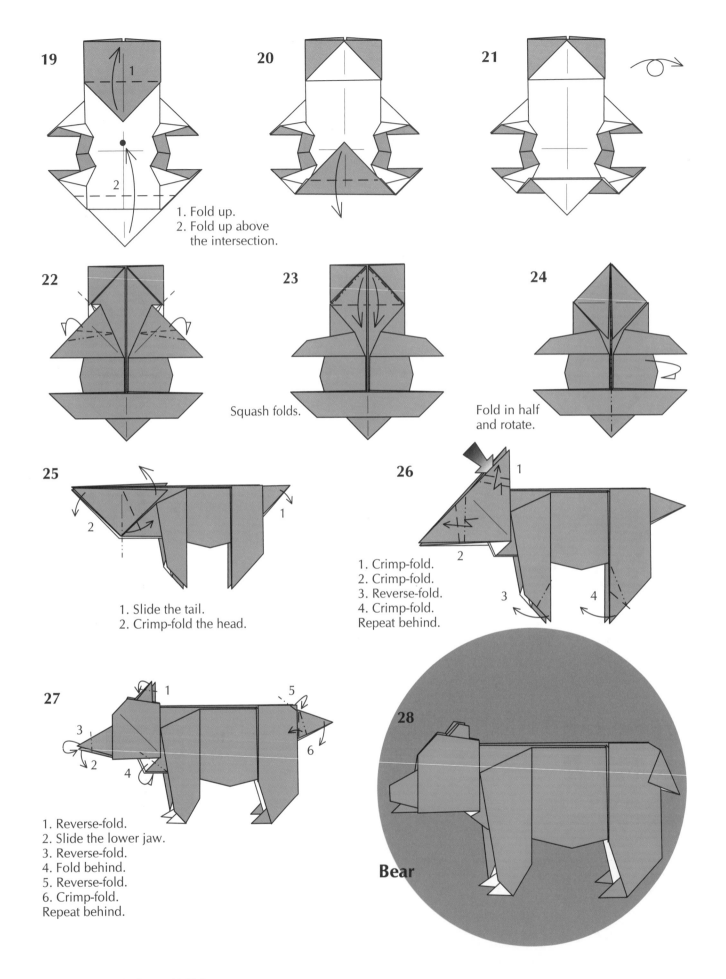

19

1. Fold up.
2. Fold up above the intersection.

20

21

22

23

Squash folds.

24

Fold in half and rotate.

25

1. Slide the tail.
2. Crimp-fold the head.

26

1. Crimp-fold.
2. Crimp-fold.
3. Reverse-fold.
4. Crimp-fold.
Repeat behind.

27

1. Reverse-fold.
2. Slide the lower jaw.
3. Reverse-fold.
4. Fold behind.
5. Reverse-fold.
6. Crimp-fold.
Repeat behind.

28

Bear

Bison

1

Fold in half.

2

Fold and unfold.
Repeat behind.

3

Fold and unfold.

4

Reverse-fold.

5

Squash-fold along the
crease. Repeat behind.

6

Repeat behind.

7

Repeat behind.

8

Fold and unfold
the top layer.
Repeat behind.

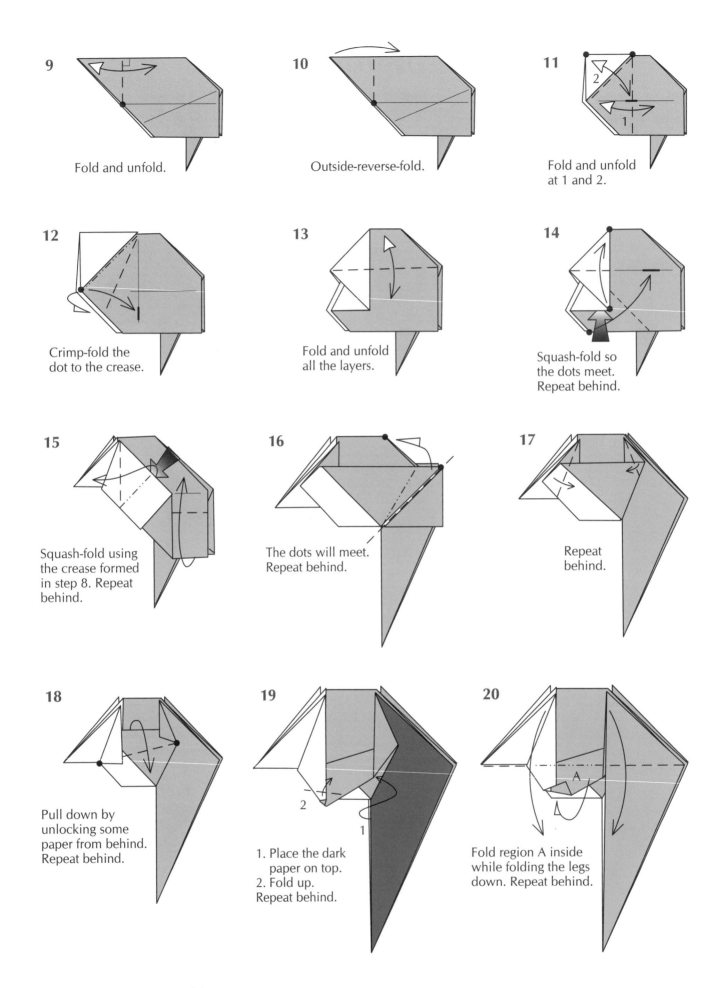

9

Fold and unfold.

10

Outside-reverse-fold.

11

Fold and unfold
at 1 and 2.

12

Crimp-fold the
dot to the crease.

13

Fold and unfold
all the layers.

14

Squash-fold so
the dots meet.
Repeat behind.

15

Squash-fold using
the crease formed
in step 8. Repeat
behind.

16

The dots will meet.
Repeat behind.

17

Repeat
behind.

18

Pull down by
unlocking some
paper from behind.
Repeat behind.

19

1. Place the dark
   paper on top.
2. Fold up.
Repeat behind.

20

Fold region A inside
while folding the legs
down. Repeat behind.

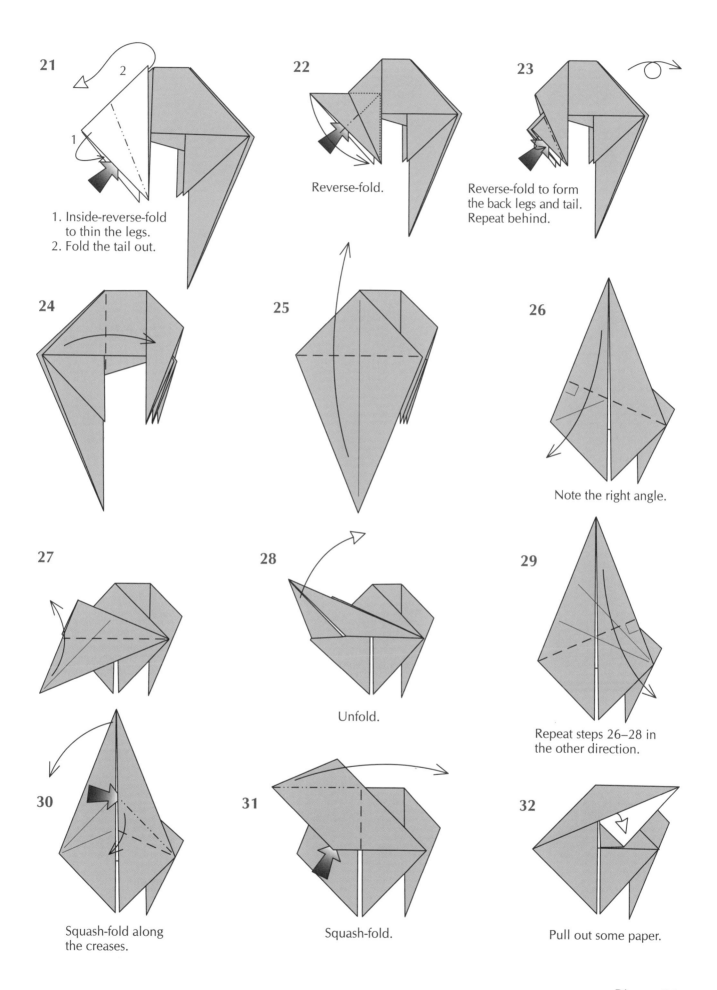

21

1. Inside-reverse-fold to thin the legs.
2. Fold the tail out.

22

Reverse-fold.

23

Reverse-fold to form the back legs and tail. Repeat behind.

24

25

26

Note the right angle.

27

28

Unfold.

29

Repeat steps 26–28 in the other direction.

30

Squash-fold along the creases.

31

Squash-fold.

32

Pull out some paper.

Bison 31

33

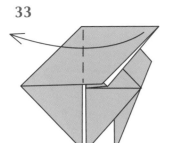

34

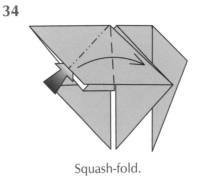

Squash-fold.

35

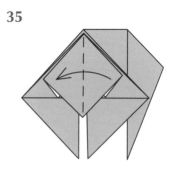

36

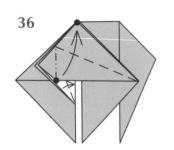

Squash-fold. The dots will meet.

37

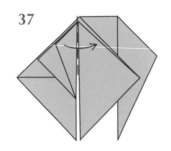

38

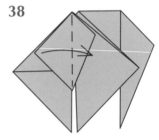

Repeat steps 35–37 on the left side.

39

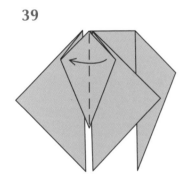

40

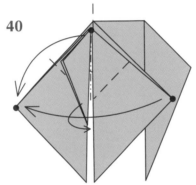

The dots will meet.

41

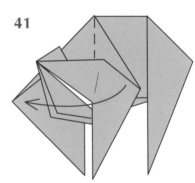

A 3D intermediate step.

42

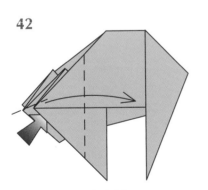

Squash-fold, repeat behind.

43

Fold one of the two layers up. Repeat behind.

44

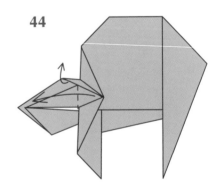

A 3D intermediate step. Repeat behind.

45

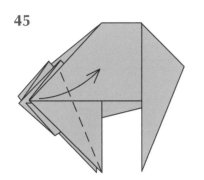

Repeat behind.

46

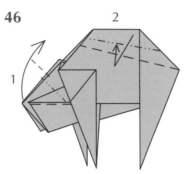

1. Crimp-fold the head.
2. Pleat-fold.

47

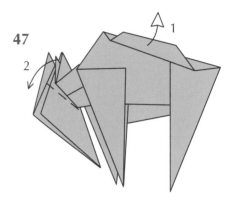

1. Unfold the back.
2. Pull out the horn
   and repeat behind.

48

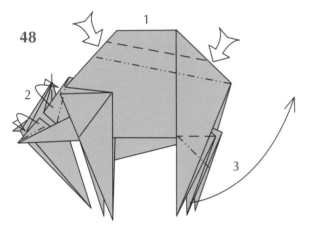

1. Sink down and up to form the back.
2. Reverse folds at the head. Repeat behind.
3. Crimp-fold the tail.

49

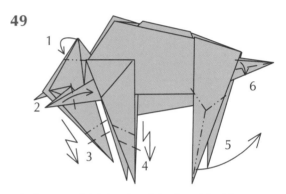

1. Reverse-fold the tip of the head inside.
2. Fold the horn to the right. Repeat behind.
3. Crimp-fold the beard.
4. Crimp-fold the front legs. Repeat behind.
5. Double-rabbit-ear the hind legs. Repeat behind.
6. Thin the tail. Repeat behind.

50

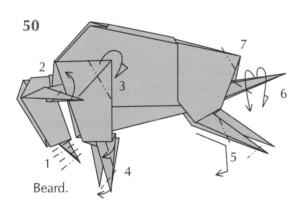

Beard.

1. Pleat the beard.
2. Outside-reverse-fold the horn up
   to make it white. Repeat behind.
3. Repeat behind.
4. Shape the front legs.
   Repeat behind for each leg.
5. Reverse folds to shape the
   hind legs. Repeat behind.
6. Outside-reverse-fold the tail.
7. Reverse-fold.

51

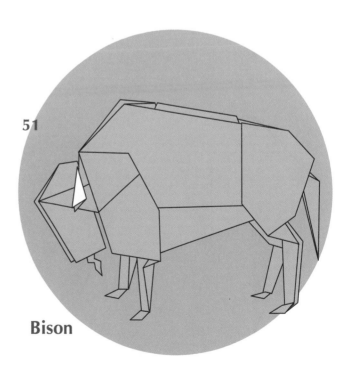

Bison

Camel

Begin with step 24 of the Bison on page 29.

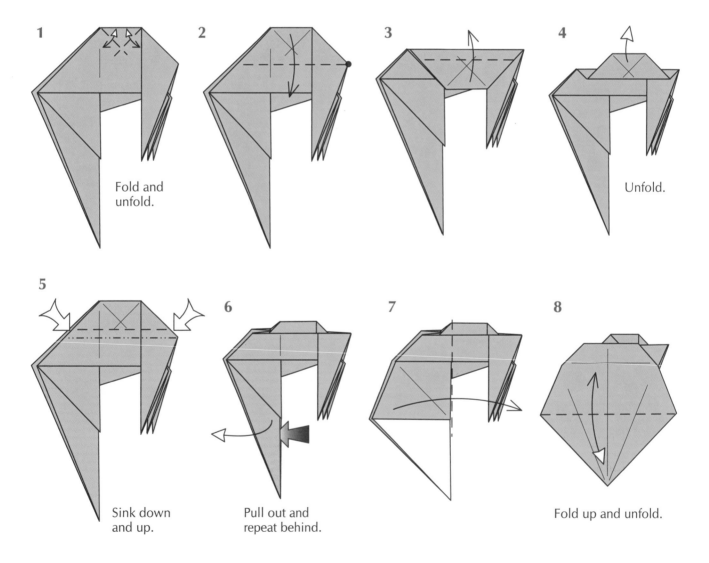

1 Fold and unfold.

2

3

4 Unfold.

5 Sink down and up.

6 Pull out and repeat behind.

7

8 Fold up and unfold.

9

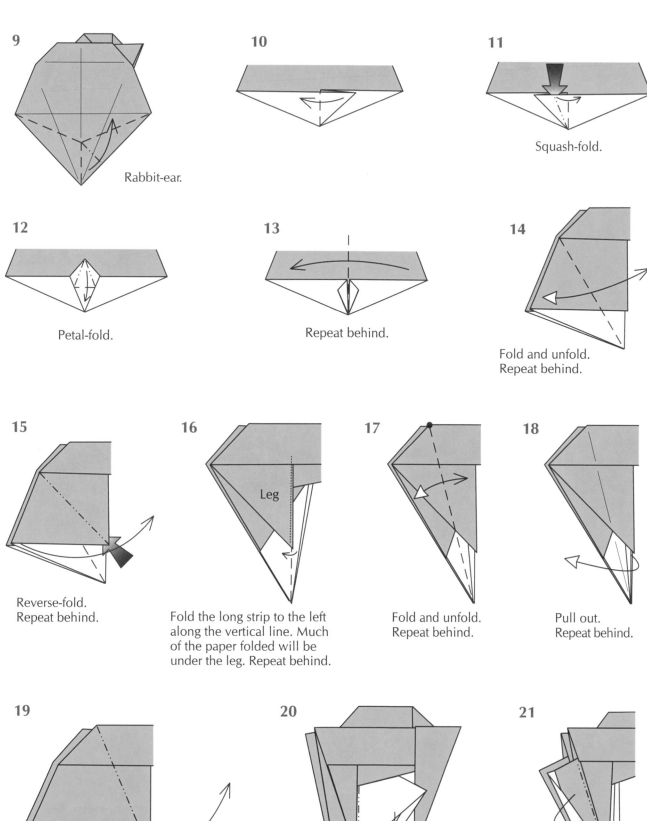

Rabbit-ear.

10

11

Squash-fold.

12

Petal-fold.

13

Repeat behind.

14

Fold and unfold.
Repeat behind.

15

Reverse-fold.
Repeat behind.

16

Leg

Fold the long strip to the left along the vertical line. Much of the paper folded will be under the leg. Repeat behind.

17

Fold and unfold.
Repeat behind.

18

Pull out.
Repeat behind.

19

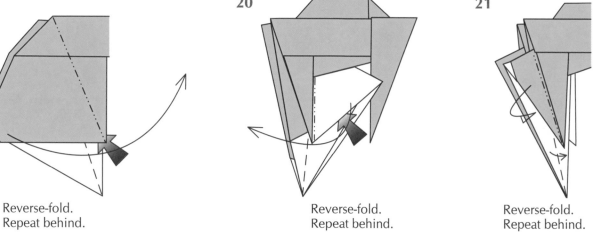

Reverse-fold.
Repeat behind.

20

Reverse-fold.
Repeat behind.

21

Reverse-fold.
Repeat behind.

22

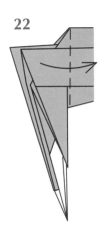

23

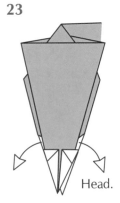

Head.

Pull out the hidden
white paper.

24

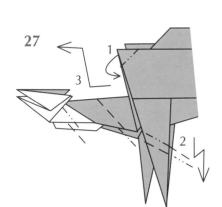

Reverse folds.

25

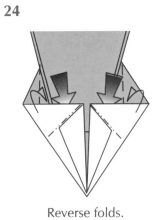

26

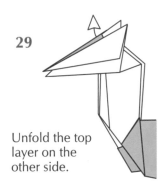

Reverse-fold.

27

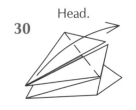

1
3
2

1. Reverse-fold. Repeat behind.
2. Crimp-fold the leg. Repeat behind.
3. Make two outside reverse folds
   for the neck and head.

28

Front leg.

Repeat behind.

29

Unfold the top
layer on the
other side.

30

Head.

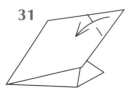

31

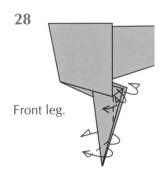

Formation
of the eyes.

32

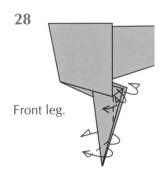

33

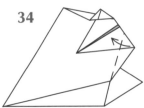

34

Repeat steps 32–33 to
form the other eye.

35

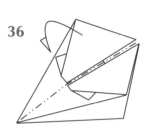

36

37

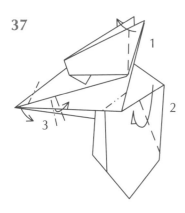

1. Fold the ear. Repeat behind.
2. Form the neck. Repeat behind.
3. Crimp-fold the mouth.

38

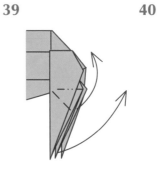

Reverse-fold.

39

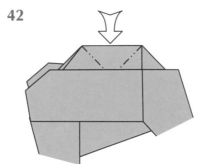

Crimp-fold to form the tail.

40

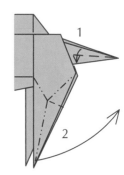

1. Thin the tail.
2. Double-rabbit-ear to form the hind leg. Repeat behind.

41

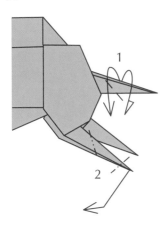

1. Outside-reverse-fold the tail.
2. Reverse folds to form the leg and hoof. Repeat behind.

42

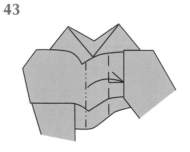

Formation of the humps.

43

This is 3D. Repeat behind.

44

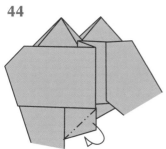

Repeat behind.

45

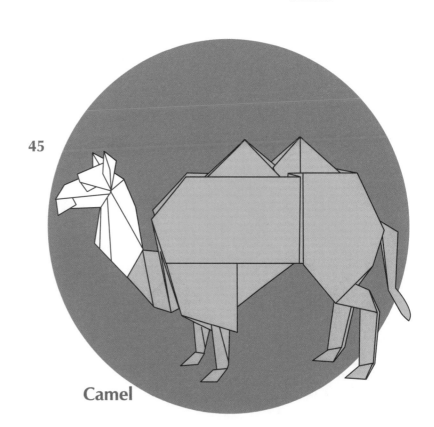

Camel

Chameleon

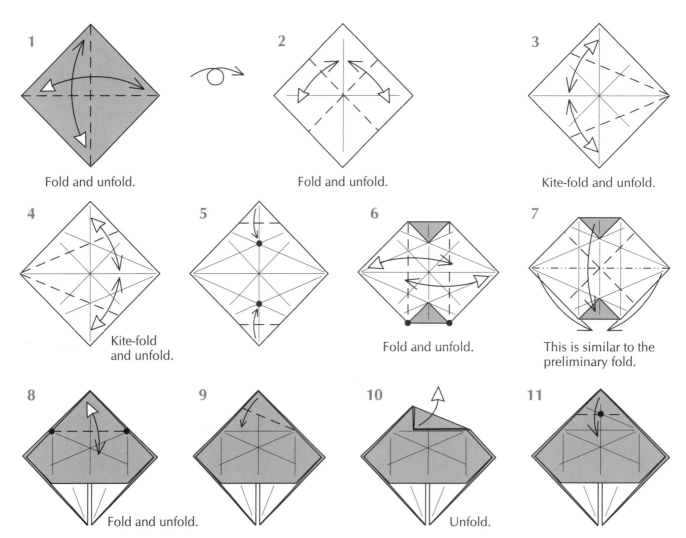

1 Fold and unfold.

2 Fold and unfold.

3 Kite-fold and unfold.

4 Kite-fold and unfold.

5

6 Fold and unfold.

7 This is similar to the preliminary fold.

8 Fold and unfold.

9

10 Unfold.

11

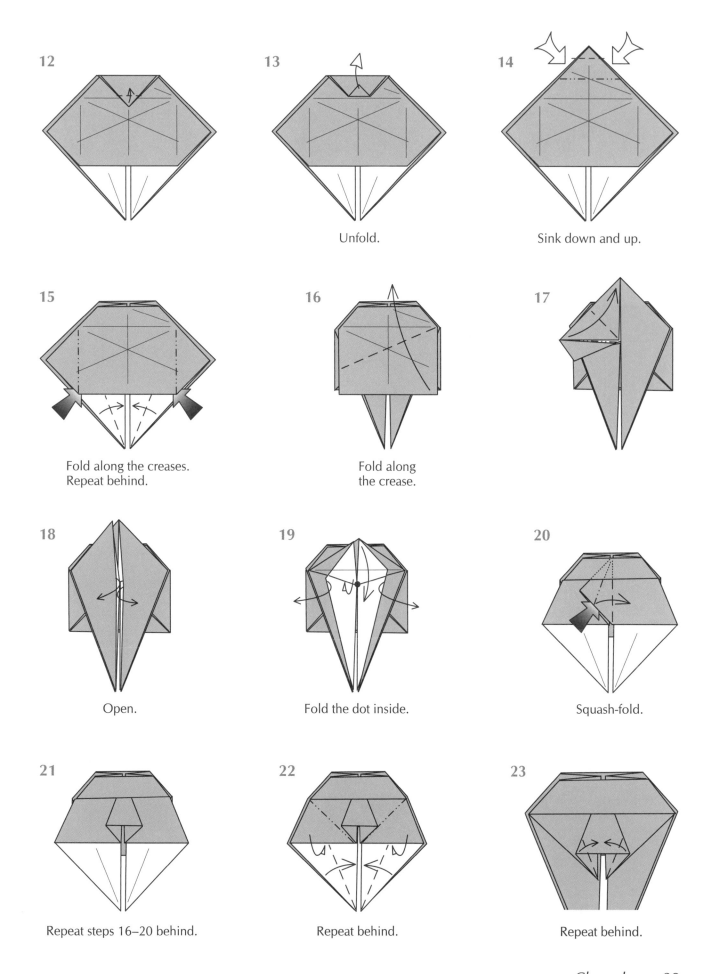

12

13

Unfold.

14

Sink down and up.

15

Fold along the creases.
Repeat behind.

16

Fold along
the crease.

17

18

Open.

19

Fold the dot inside.

20

Squash-fold.

21

Repeat steps 16–20 behind.

22

Repeat behind.

23

Repeat behind.

Chameleon 39

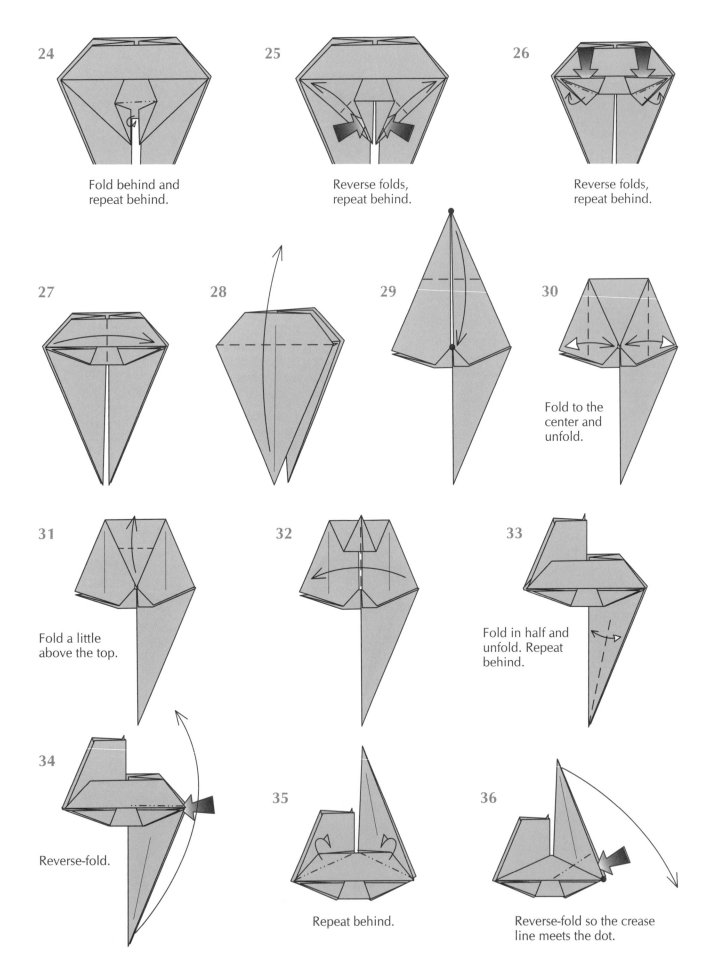

24 Fold behind and repeat behind.

25 Reverse folds, repeat behind.

26 Reverse folds, repeat behind.

27

28

29

30 Fold to the center and unfold.

31 Fold a little above the top.

32

33 Fold in half and unfold. Repeat behind.

34 Reverse-fold.

35 Repeat behind.

36 Reverse-fold so the crease line meets the dot.

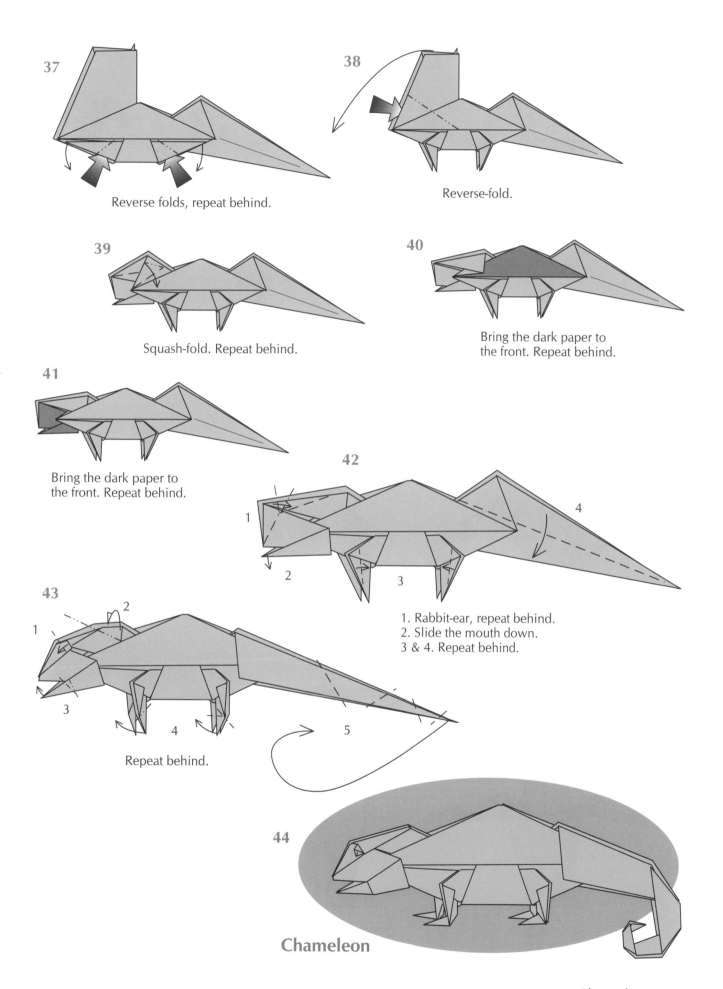

37

Reverse folds, repeat behind.

38

Reverse-fold.

39

Squash-fold. Repeat behind.

40

Bring the dark paper to
the front. Repeat behind.

41

Bring the dark paper to
the front. Repeat behind.

42

1. Rabbit-ear, repeat behind.
2. Slide the mouth down.
3 & 4. Repeat behind.

43

Repeat behind.

44

Chameleon

Chimpanzee

Begin with step 64 of the Gorilla on page 66.

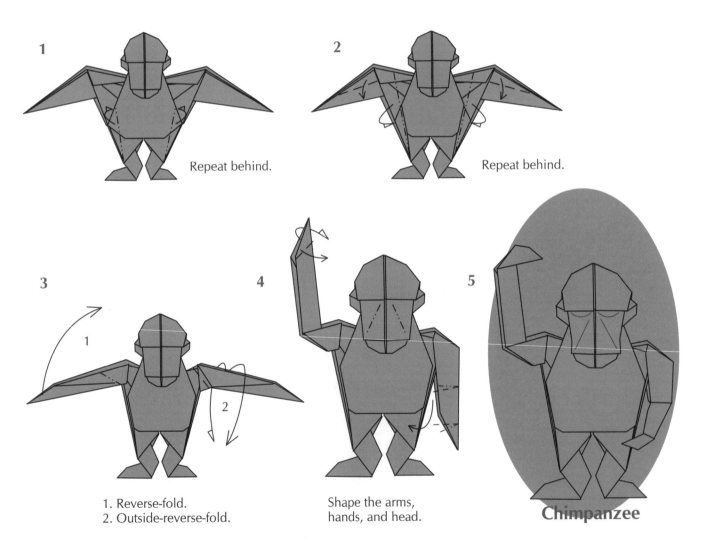

1

Repeat behind.

2

Repeat behind.

3

1. Reverse-fold.
2. Outside-reverse-fold.

4

Shape the arms,
hands, and head.

5

Chimpanzee

Simple Crocodile

1
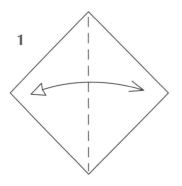
Fold and unfold.

2
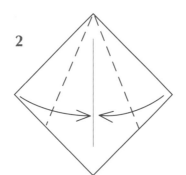
Fold to the center.

3
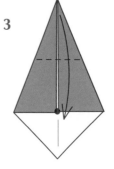
Fold down a little below the dot.

4
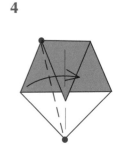

5
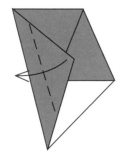

6
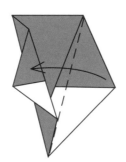
Repeat steps 4–5 on the right.

7

Pull out the hidden flap.

8
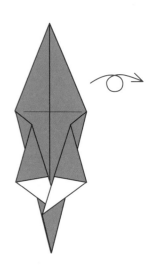

9

Pleat folds.

10
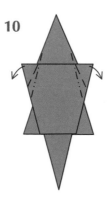
Pleat folds.

11
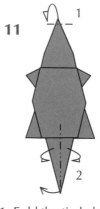
1. Fold the tip behind.
2. Bend and curl the tail a little bit.

12
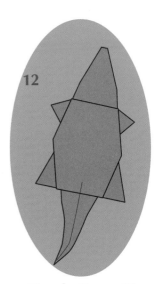
Simple Crocodile

Crocodile

1

Fold and unfold.

2

Fold and unfold
on the edge.

3

Fold and unfold
on the diagonal.

4

5

6

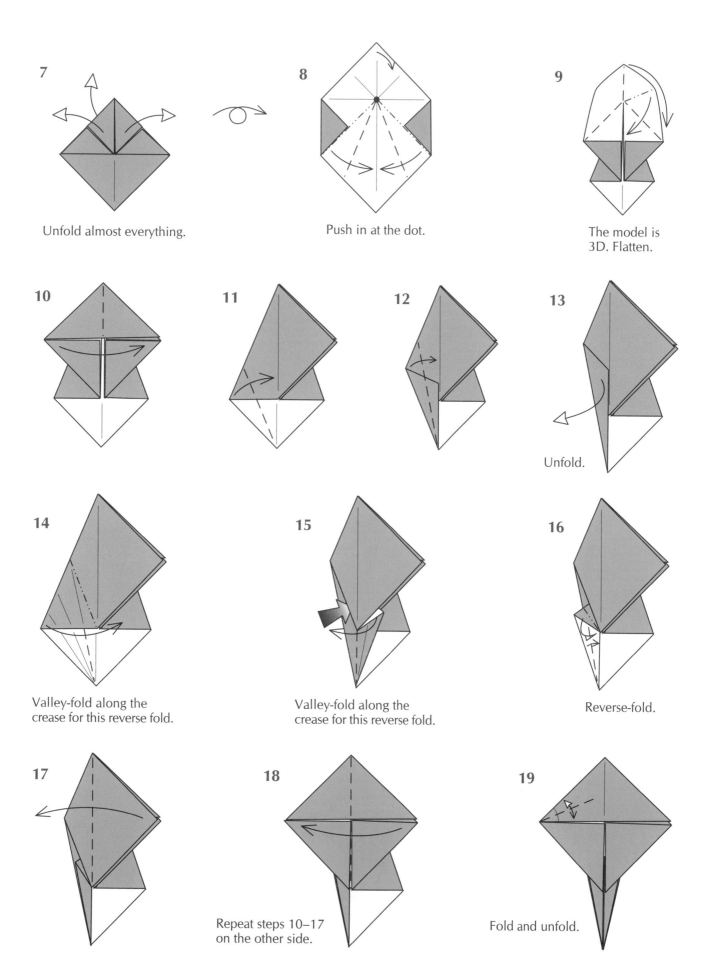

7 Unfold almost everything.

8 Push in at the dot.

9 The model is 3D. Flatten.

10

11

12

13 Unfold.

14 Valley-fold along the crease for this reverse fold.

15 Valley-fold along the crease for this reverse fold.

16 Reverse-fold.

17

18 Repeat steps 10–17 on the other side.

19 Fold and unfold.

Crocodile 45

20

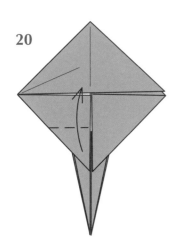

21

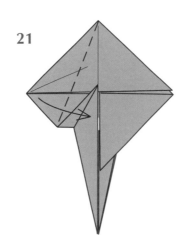

22

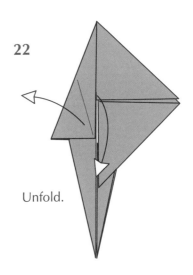

Unfold.

23

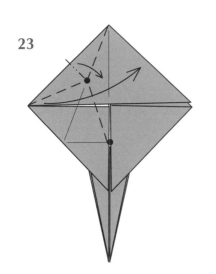

24

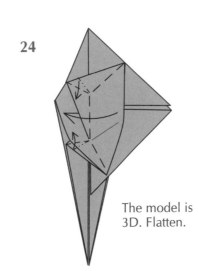

The model is
3D. Flatten.

25

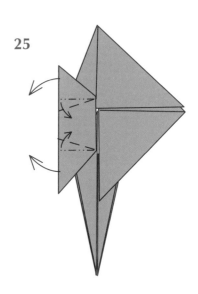

26

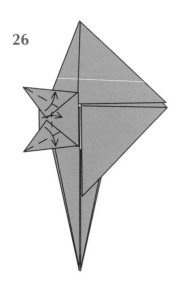

27

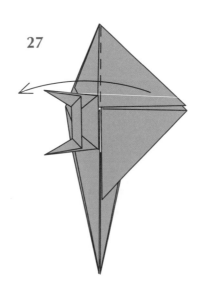

28

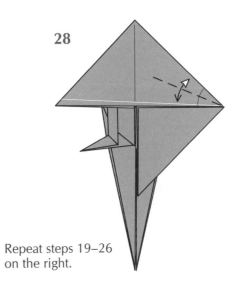

Repeat steps 19–26
on the right.

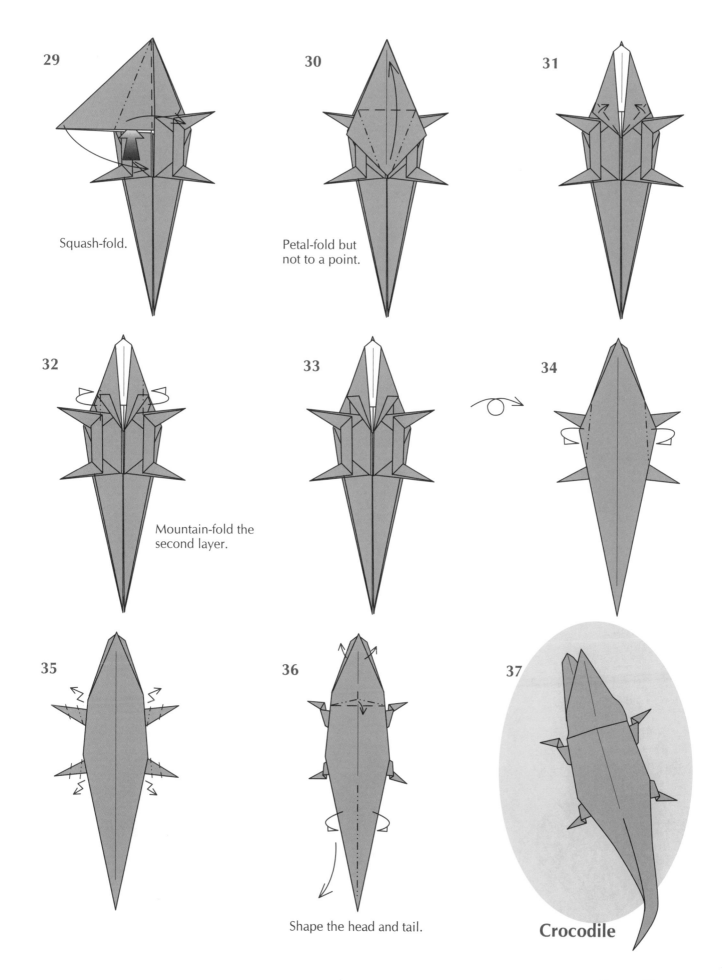

29 Squash-fold.

30 Petal-fold but not to a point.

31

32 Mountain-fold the second layer.

33

34

35

36 Shape the head and tail.

37 **Crocodile**

Dromedary

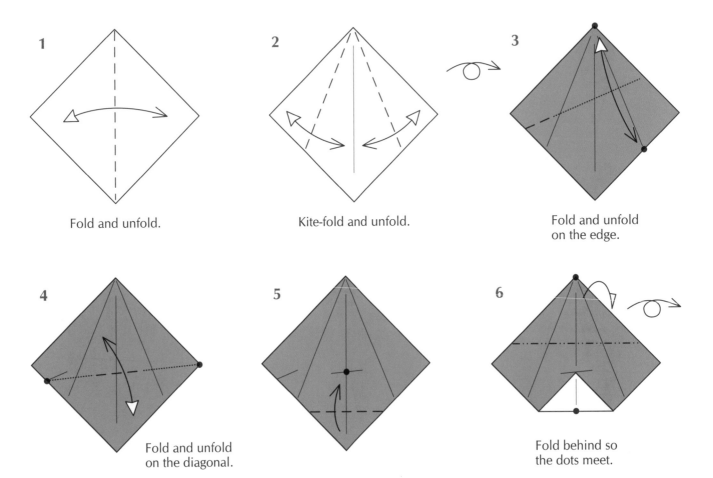

1 Fold and unfold.

2 Kite-fold and unfold.

3 Fold and unfold on the edge.

4 Fold and unfold on the diagonal.

5

6 Fold behind so the dots meet.

7

8

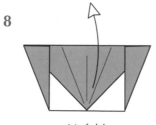

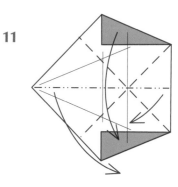

Unfold.

9

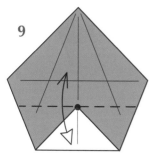

Fold and unfold.
Rotate.

10

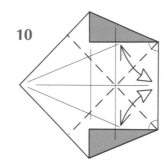

Fold and unfold.

11

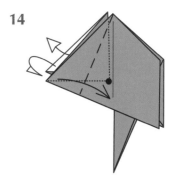

Collapse along the creases.

12

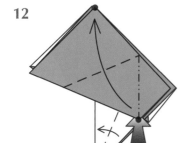

Squash-fold along the
creases. Repeat behind.

13

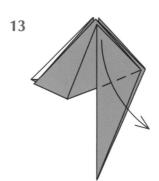

Repeat behind.

14

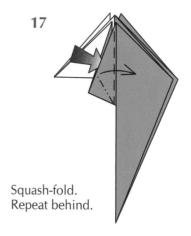

Pull out the corner with
the dot while folding along
the valley line, repeat
behind at the same time.

15

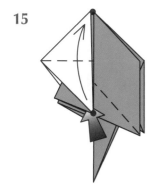

Squash-fold so the dots
meet. Repeat behind.

16

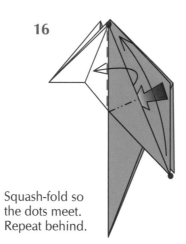

Squash-fold so
the dots meet.
Repeat behind.

17

Squash-fold.
Repeat behind.

18

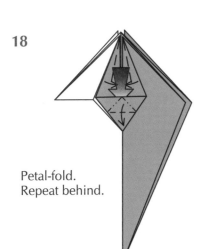

Petal-fold.
Repeat behind.

19

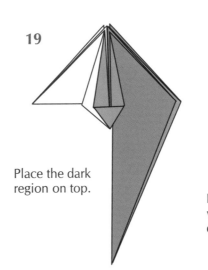

Place the dark
region on top.

20

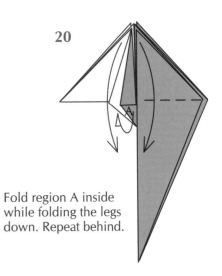

Fold region A inside
while folding the legs
down. Repeat behind.

21

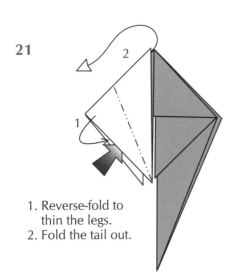

1. Reverse-fold to
   thin the legs.
2. Fold the tail out.

22

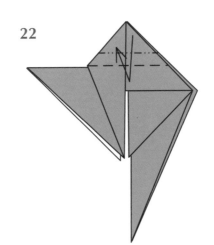

23

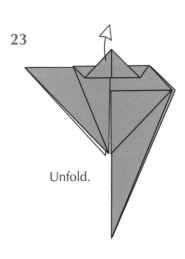

Unfold.

24

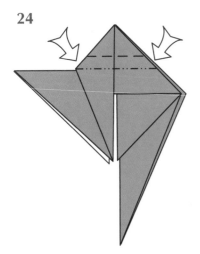

Sink down and up along the
creases to form the hump.

25

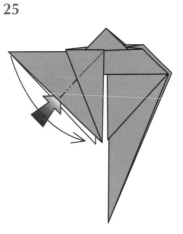

Reverse-fold.

26

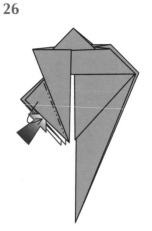

Reverse-fold,
repeat behind.

27

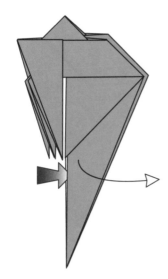

Continue with step 6 of the camel (page 34) through the end but omit the folds dealing with the humps or front legs.

28

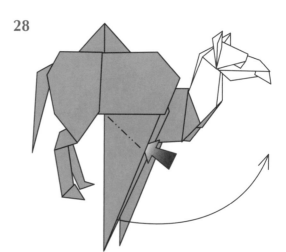

Reverse-fold.
Repeat behind.

29

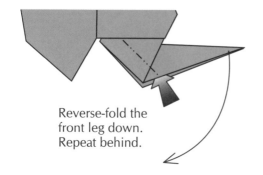

Reverse-fold the front leg down.
Repeat behind.

30

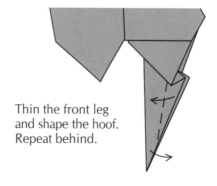

Thin the front leg and shape the hoof.
Repeat behind.

31

Dromedary

African Elephant

1

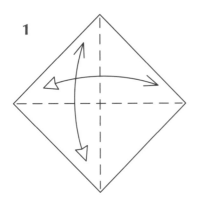

Fold and unfold.

2

Fold and unfold
on the edge.

3

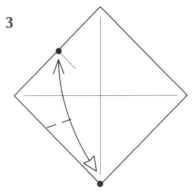

Fold and unfold
on the left.

4

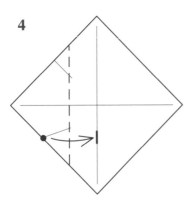

5

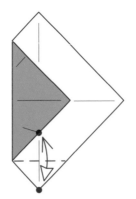

Fold and unfold.

6

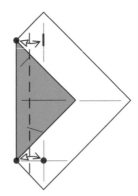

Fold and unfold
to the center.

7

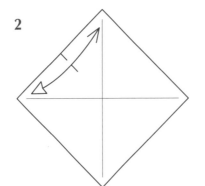

Fold and unfold
the top layer.

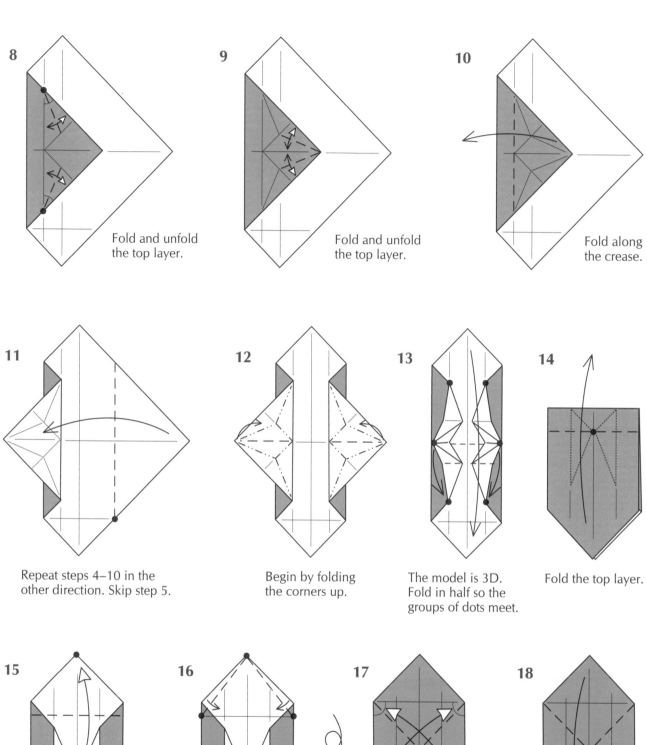

8 Fold and unfold the top layer.

9 Fold and unfold the top layer.

10 Fold along the crease.

11 Repeat steps 4–10 in the other direction. Skip step 5.

12 Begin by folding the corners up.

13 The model is 3D. Fold in half so the groups of dots meet.

14 Fold the top layer.

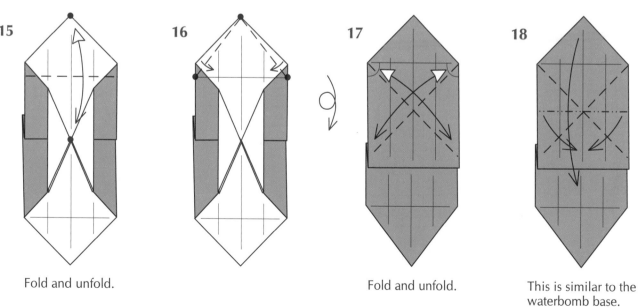

15 Fold and unfold.

16

17 Fold and unfold.

18 This is similar to the waterbomb base.

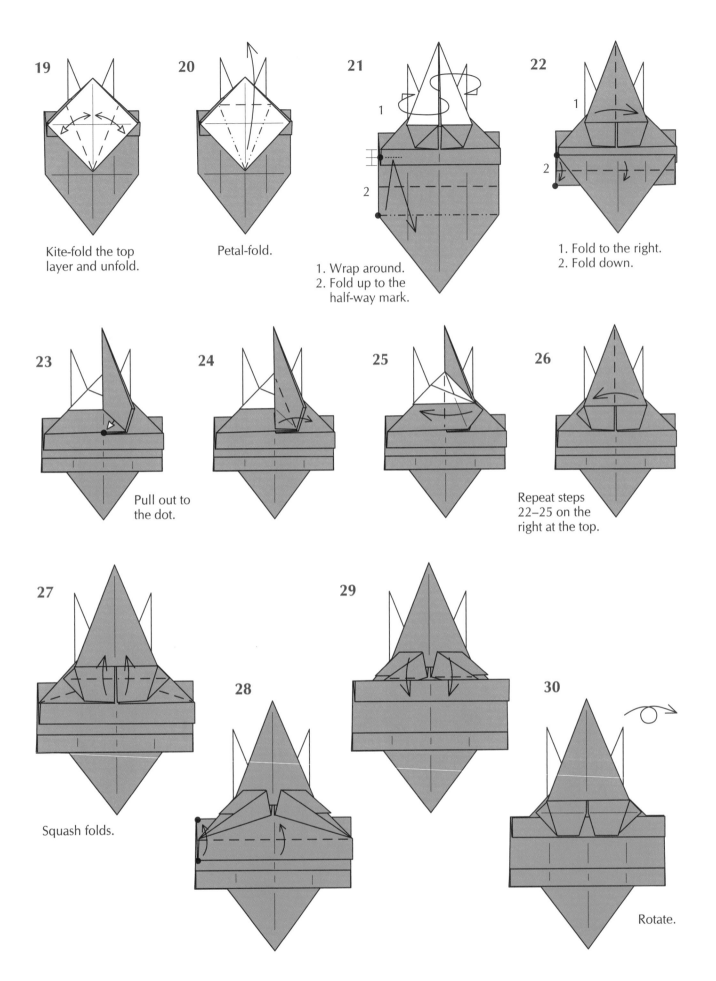

19

Kite-fold the top layer and unfold.

20

Petal-fold.

21

1. Wrap around.
2. Fold up to the half-way mark.

22

1. Fold to the right.
2. Fold down.

23

Pull out to the dot.

24

25

26

Repeat steps 22–25 on the right at the top.

27

Squash folds.

28

29

30

Rotate.

31

1. Petal-fold.
2. Pleat-fold.

32

1. Petal-fold.
2. Squash-fold at an angle of 1/3.

33

Unwrap the top layer.

34

1. Tuck inside.
2. Repeat steps 31–34 on the top.

35

Fold in half.

36

Reverse folds.

37

Repeat behind.

38

1. Outside-reverse-fold.
2. Repeat behind.
3. Reverse-fold.

39

1. Fold inside.
2. Shape the ears.
3. Shape the legs.
4. Shape the back.

40

African Elephant

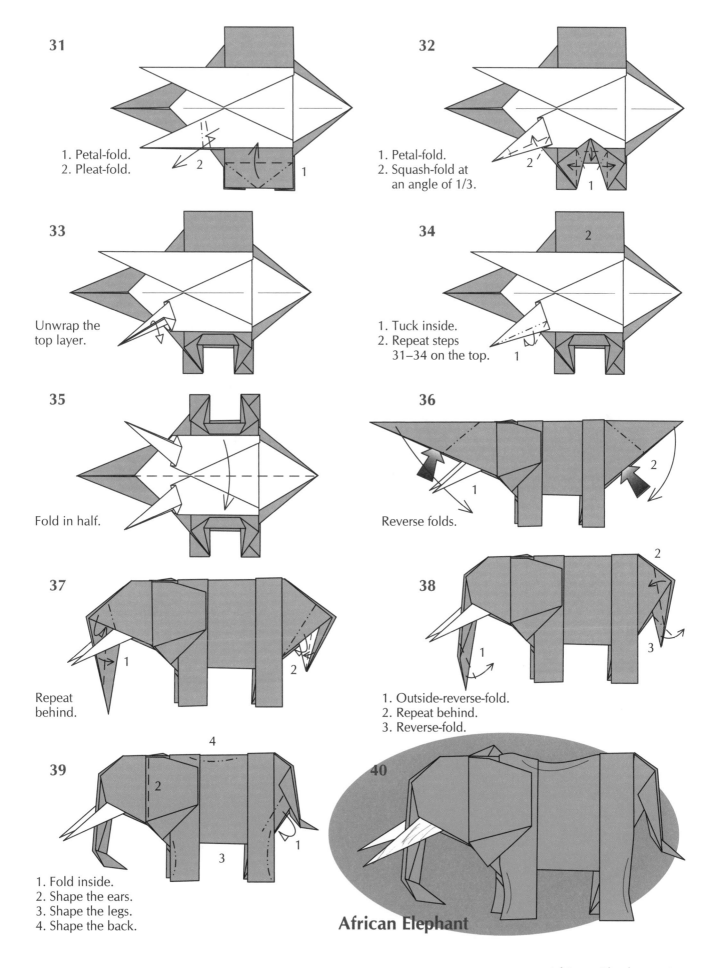

Fox

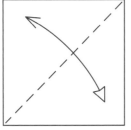

1 Fold and unfold.

2 Fold and unfold on the left.

3 Bring the corner to the crease. Fold on the left.

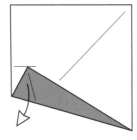

4 Unfold and rotate.

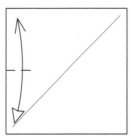

5

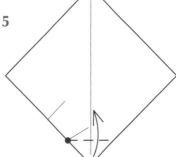

6

7

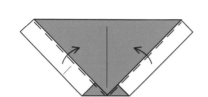

8

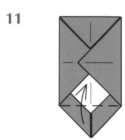

Unfold.

9

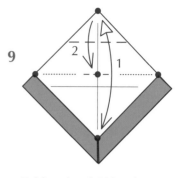

1. Fold and unfold by the center.
2. Fold down to the new crease.

10

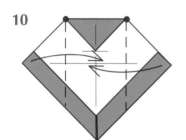

11

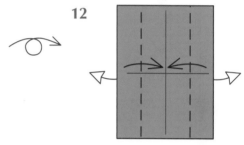

12

Fold to the center and swing out from behind.

13

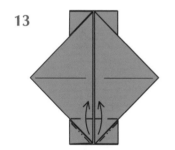

Note that the bottom layers are thicker. Make squash folds.

14

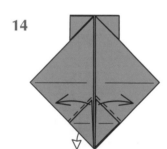

Spread.

15

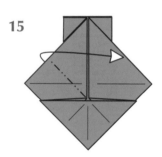

Pull out.

16

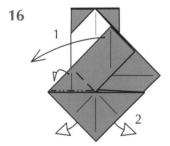

1. Refold back to step 15.
2. Unfold.

17

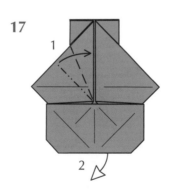

1. Mountain-fold along the crease.
2. Unfold.

18

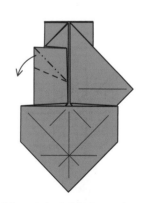

Mountain-fold along the crease for this squash fold.

Fox 57

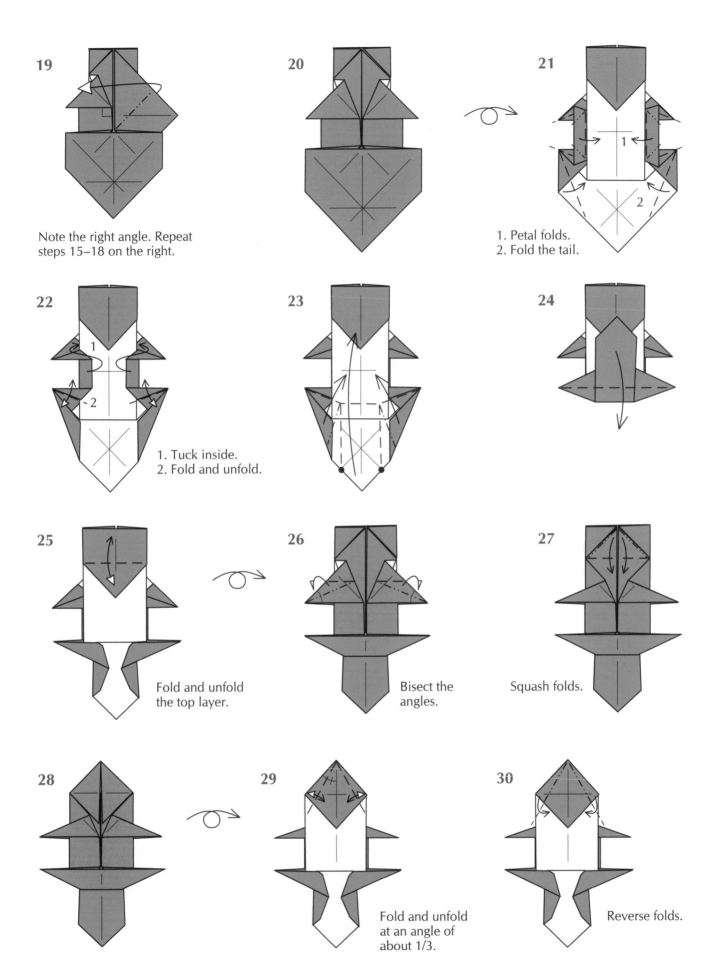

19

Note the right angle. Repeat steps 15–18 on the right.

20

21

1. Petal folds.
2. Fold the tail.

22

1. Tuck inside.
2. Fold and unfold.

23

24

25

Fold and unfold the top layer.

26

Bisect the angles.

27

Squash folds.

28

29

Fold and unfold at an angle of about 1/3.

30

Reverse folds.

31

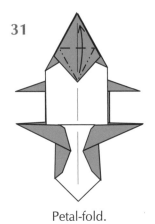

Petal-fold.

32

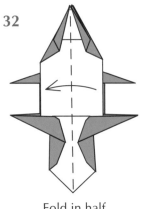

Fold in half
and rotate.

33

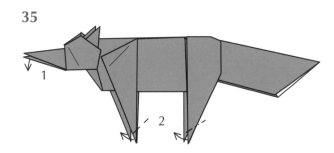

1. Crimp-fold.
2. Slide the tail.

34

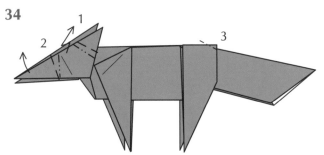

1. Pleat-fold all the layers to form
   the ears. Do not reverse fold.
   Repeat behind.
2. Crimp-fold.
3. Make a small reverse fold.

35

1. Separate the lower jaw.
2. Form the feet.
   Repeat behind.

36

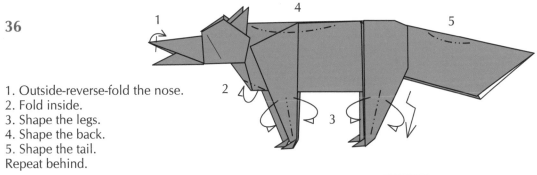

1. Outside-reverse-fold the nose.
2. Fold inside.
3. Shape the legs.
4. Shape the back.
5. Shape the tail.
Repeat behind.

37

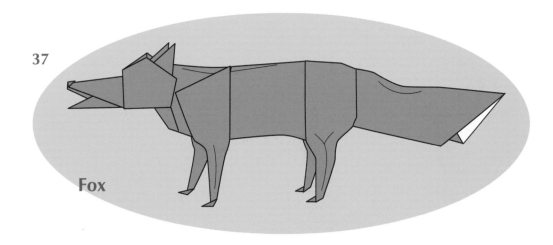

Fox

Giraffe

1

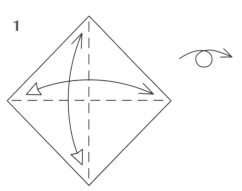

Fold and unfold.

2

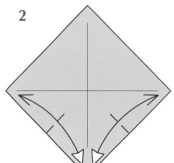

Fold and unfold
by the edges.

3

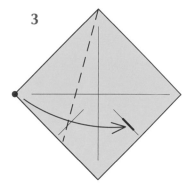

Fold the corner
to the line.

4

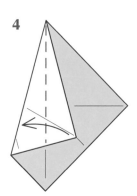

5

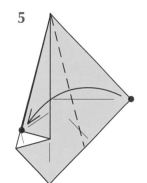

6

7

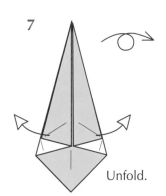

Unfold.

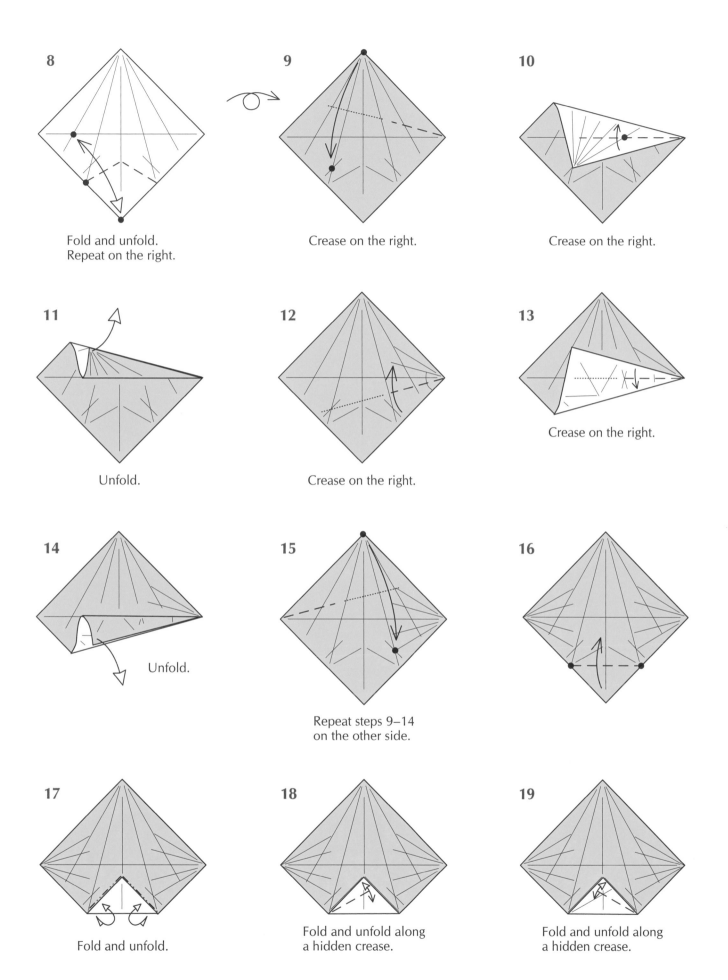

8

Fold and unfold.
Repeat on the right.

9

Crease on the right.

10

Crease on the right.

11

Unfold.

12

Crease on the right.

13

Crease on the right.

14

Unfold.

15

Repeat steps 9–14
on the other side.

16

17

Fold and unfold.

18

Fold and unfold along
a hidden crease.

19

Fold and unfold along
a hidden crease.

Giraffe 61

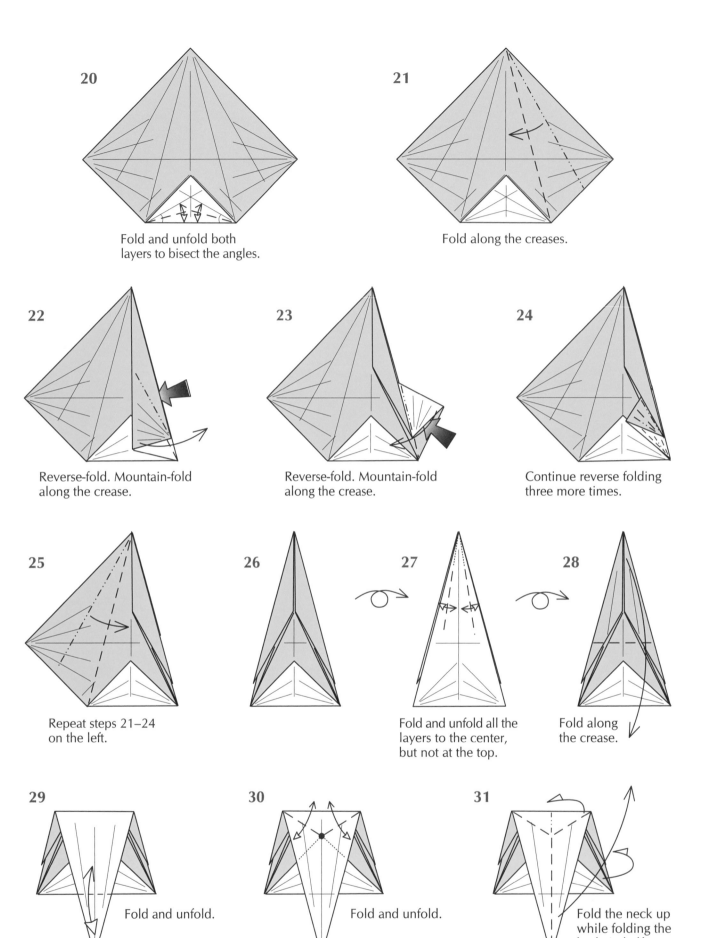

20

Fold and unfold both
layers to bisect the angles.

21

Fold along the creases.

22

Reverse-fold. Mountain-fold
along the crease.

23

Reverse-fold. Mountain-fold
along the crease.

24

Continue reverse folding
three more times.

25

Repeat steps 21–24
on the left.

26

27

Fold and unfold all the
layers to the center,
but not at the top.

28

Fold along
the crease.

29

Fold and unfold.

30

Fold and unfold.

31

Fold the neck up
while folding the
body in half.

32

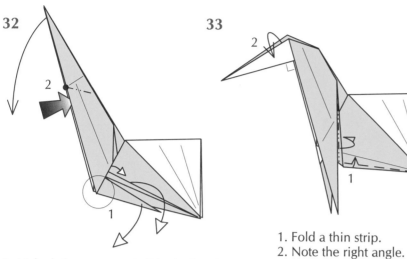

1. Unlock the paper and slide the leg down. Small, hidden, spread-squash folds will happen by the circle. Repeat behind.
2. Reverse-fold.

33

1. Fold a thin strip.
2. Note the right angle. Wrap around from inside.
Repeat behind.

34

1. Mountain-fold along the crease for this (very thin) pleat fold.
2. Pull out.
Repeat behind.

35

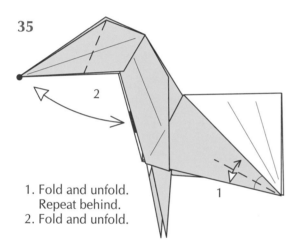

1. Fold and unfold. Repeat behind.
2. Fold and unfold.

36

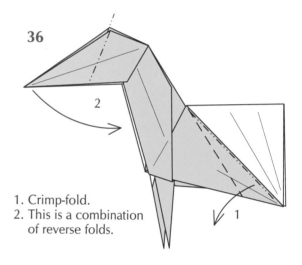

1. Crimp-fold.
2. This is a combination of reverse folds.

37

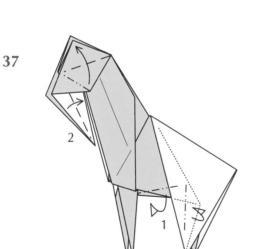

1. Thin the leg on the inside.
2. Squash-fold.
Repeat behind.

38

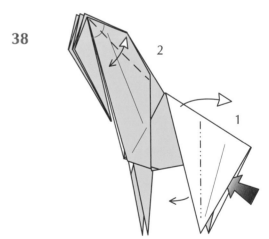

1. Reverse-fold along the crease and pivot at the tail.
2. Fold and unfold the top layers.
Repeat behind.

39

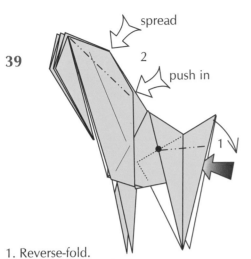

spread

2

push in

1

1. Reverse-fold.
2. Sink. Push in at the lower arrow
   and spread while sinking at the
   upper arrow. Repeat behind.

40

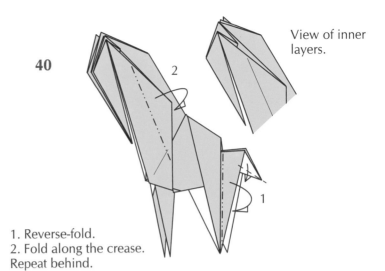

2

View of inner
layers.

1

1. Reverse-fold.
2. Fold along the crease.
   Repeat behind.

41

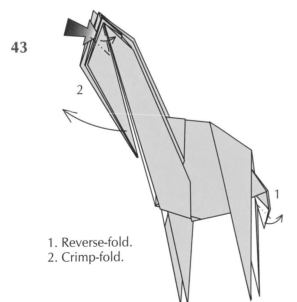

2

1

1. Reverse-fold.
2. Sink along the crease.
   Spread much of the
   model to do this sink.

42

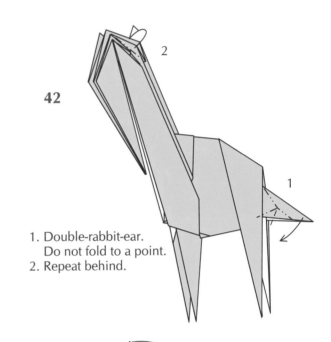

2

1

1. Double-rabbit-ear.
   Do not fold to a point.
2. Repeat behind.

43

2

1

1. Reverse-fold.
2. Crimp-fold.

44

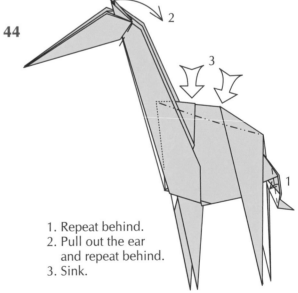

2

3

1

1. Repeat behind.
2. Pull out the ear
   and repeat behind.
3. Sink.

45

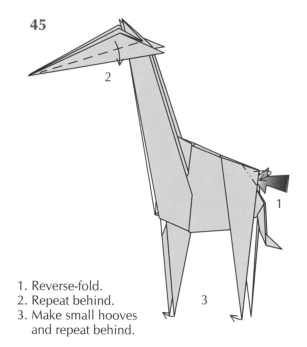

1. Reverse-fold.
2. Repeat behind.
3. Make small hooves
   and repeat behind.

46

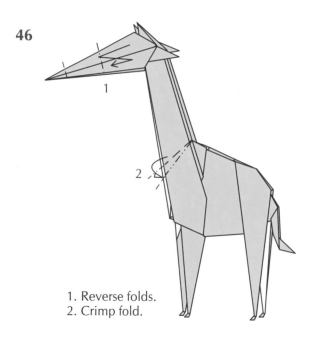

1. Reverse folds.
2. Crimp fold.

47

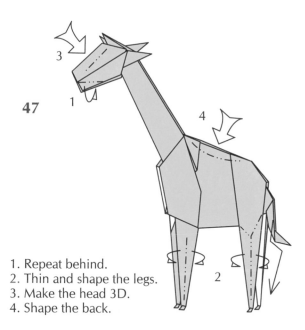

1. Repeat behind.
2. Thin and shape the legs.
3. Make the head 3D.
4. Shape the back.

48

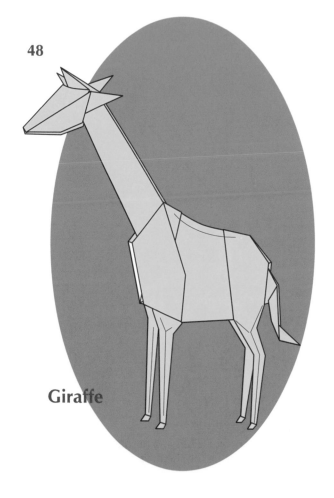

Giraffe

Gorilla

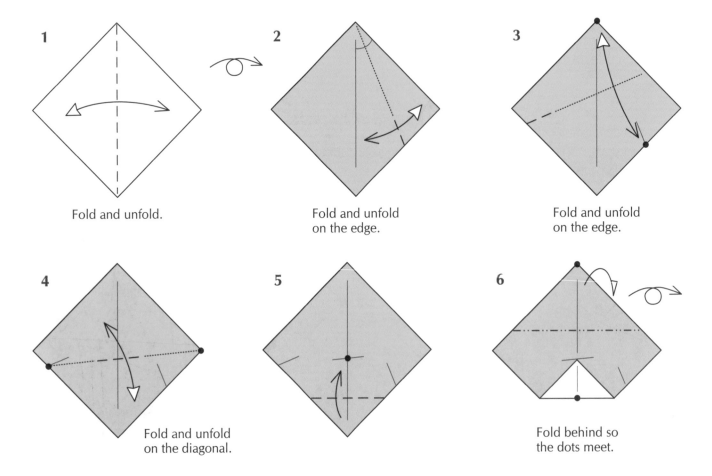

1

Fold and unfold.

2

Fold and unfold
on the edge.

3

Fold and unfold
on the edge.

4

Fold and unfold
on the diagonal.

5

6

Fold behind so
the dots meet.

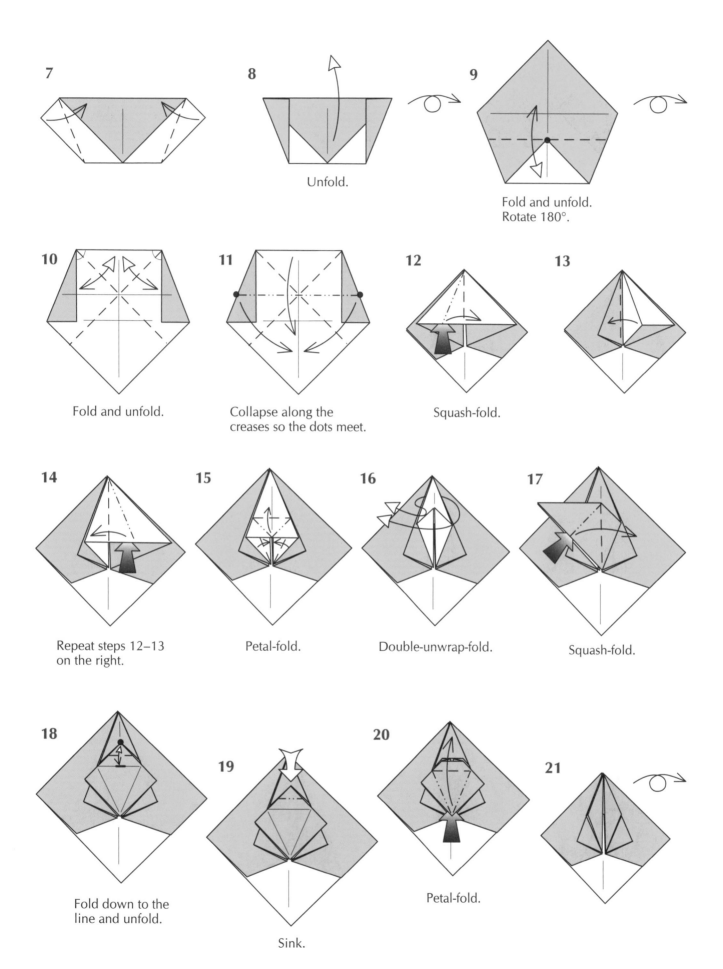

7

8

Unfold.

9

Fold and unfold.
Rotate 180°.

10

Fold and unfold.

11

Collapse along the
creases so the dots meet.

12

Squash-fold.

13

14

Repeat steps 12–13
on the right.

15

Petal-fold.

16

Double-unwrap-fold.

17

Squash-fold.

18

Fold down to the
line and unfold.

19

Sink.

20

Petal-fold.

21

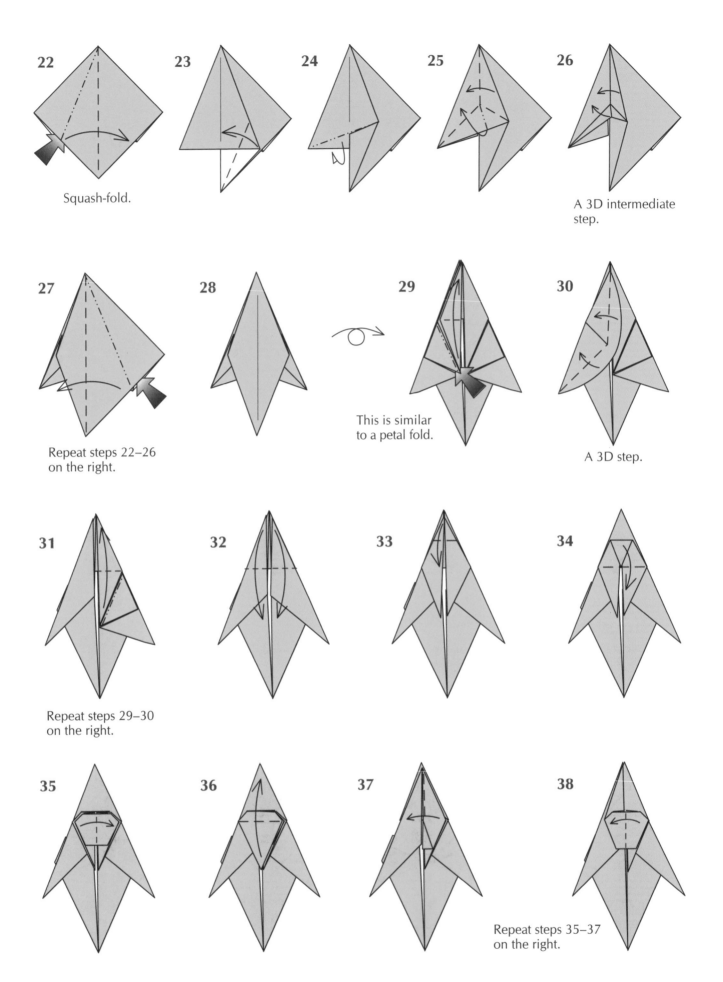

22

Squash-fold.

23

24

25

26

A 3D intermediate step.

27

Repeat steps 22–26 on the right.

28

29

This is similar to a petal fold.

30

A 3D step.

31

Repeat steps 29–30 on the right.

32

33

34

35

36

37

38

Repeat steps 35–37 on the right.

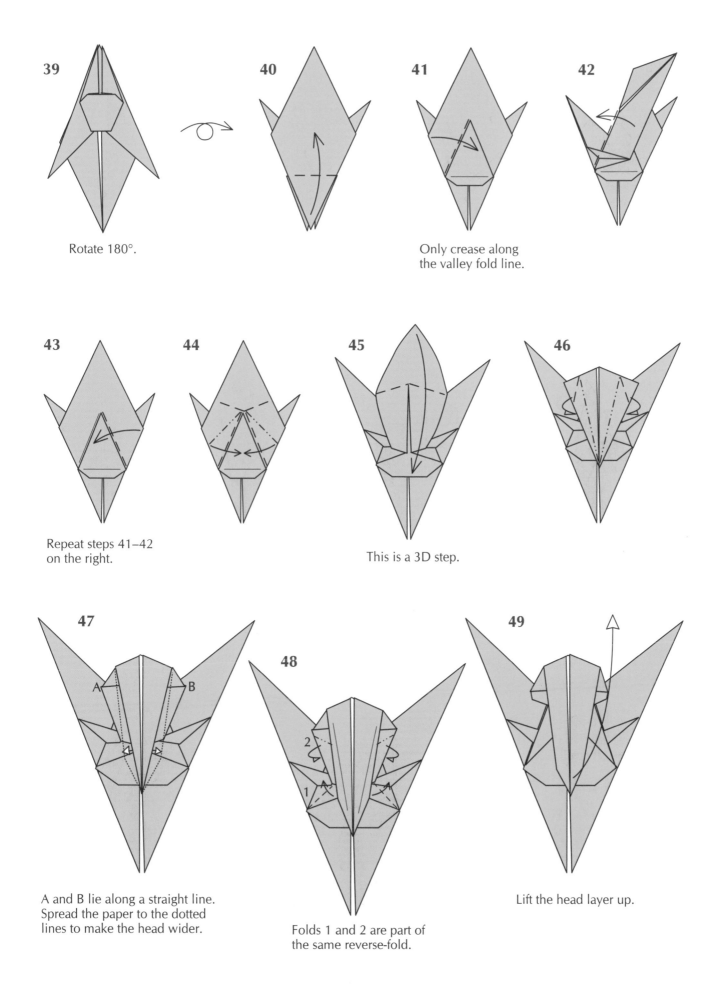

39

Rotate 180°.

40

41

Only crease along
the valley fold line.

42

43

Repeat steps 41–42
on the right.

44

45

This is a 3D step.

46

47

A and B lie along a straight line.
Spread the paper to the dotted
lines to make the head wider.

48

Folds 1 and 2 are part of
the same reverse-fold.

49

Lift the head layer up.

Gorilla 69

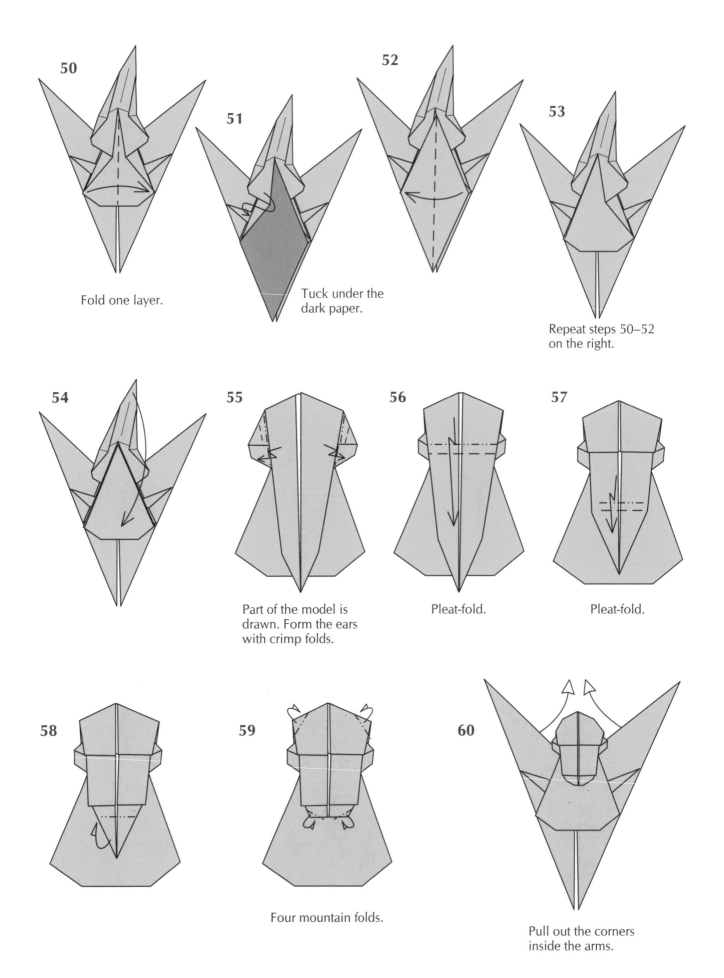

50

Fold one layer.

51

Tuck under the dark paper.

52

53

Repeat steps 50–52 on the right.

54

55

Part of the model is drawn. Form the ears with crimp folds.

56

Pleat-fold.

57

Pleat-fold.

58

59

Four mountain folds.

60

Pull out the corners inside the arms.

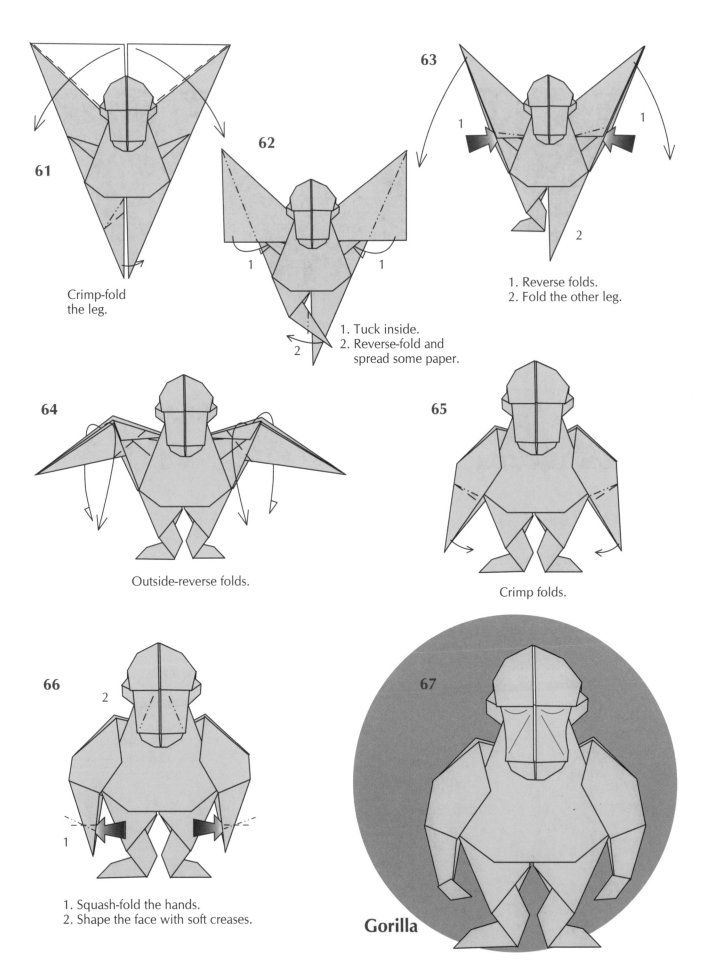

61

Crimp-fold
the leg.

62

1. Tuck inside.
2. Reverse-fold and
spread some paper.

63

1. Reverse folds.
2. Fold the other leg.

64

Outside-reverse folds.

65

Crimp folds.

66

1. Squash-fold the hands.
2. Shape the face with soft creases.

67

Gorilla

Hippopotamus

1

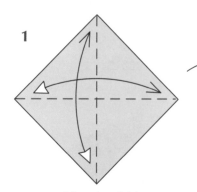

Fold and unfold.

2

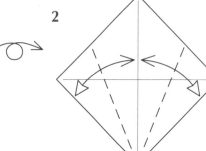

Kite-fold and unfold.

3

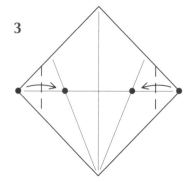

4

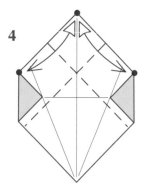

Fold and unfold.

5

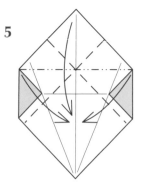

This is similar to the
preliminary fold.

6

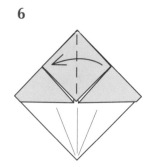

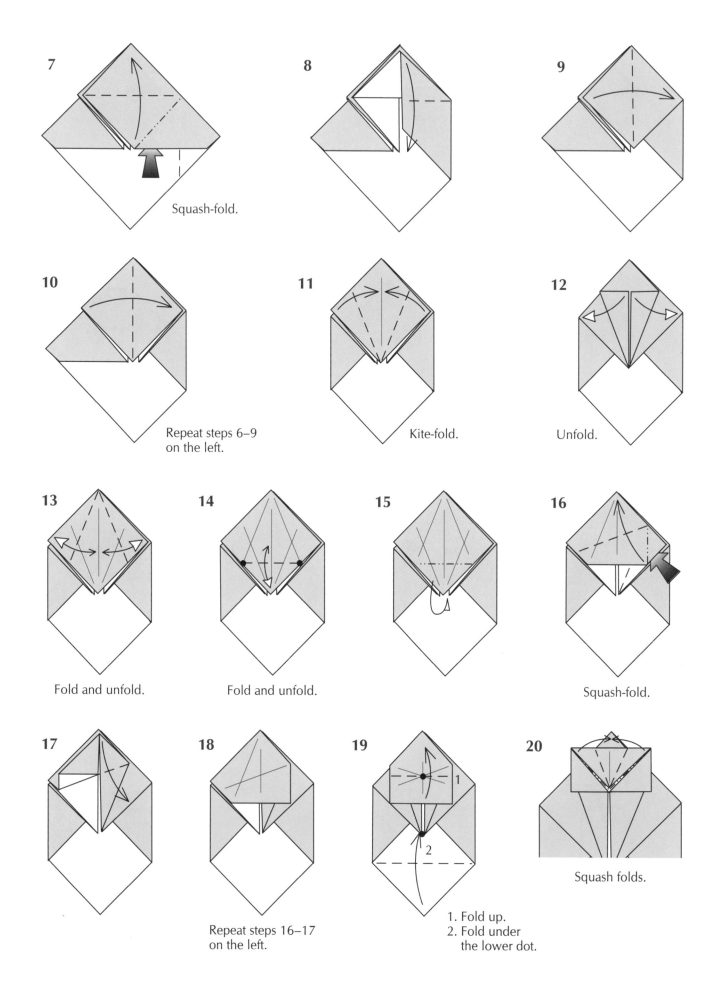

7

Squash-fold.

8

9

10

Repeat steps 6–9
on the left.

11

Kite-fold.

12

Unfold.

13

Fold and unfold.

14

Fold and unfold.

15

16

Squash-fold.

17

18

Repeat steps 16–17
on the left.

19

1. Fold up.
2. Fold under
   the lower dot.

20

Squash folds.

21

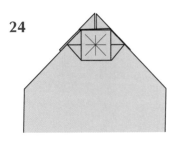

22

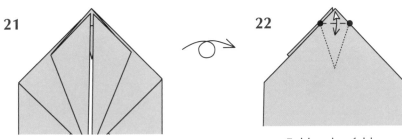

Fold and unfold.

23

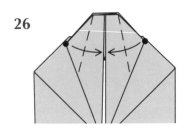

Spread-squash-fold.
Mountain-fold along
the crease.

24

25

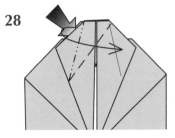

Reverse folds.

26

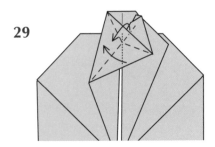

Fold the corners
to the center.

27

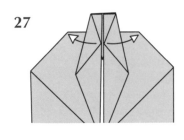

Unfold.

28

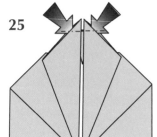

Spread-squash-fold.

29

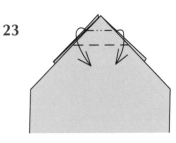

30

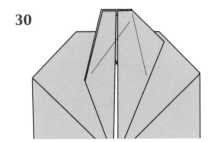

Repeat steps 28–29
on the right.

31

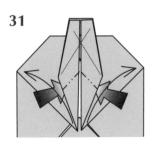

Reverse folds.

32

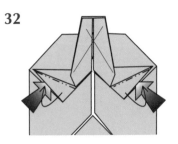

Reverse folds.

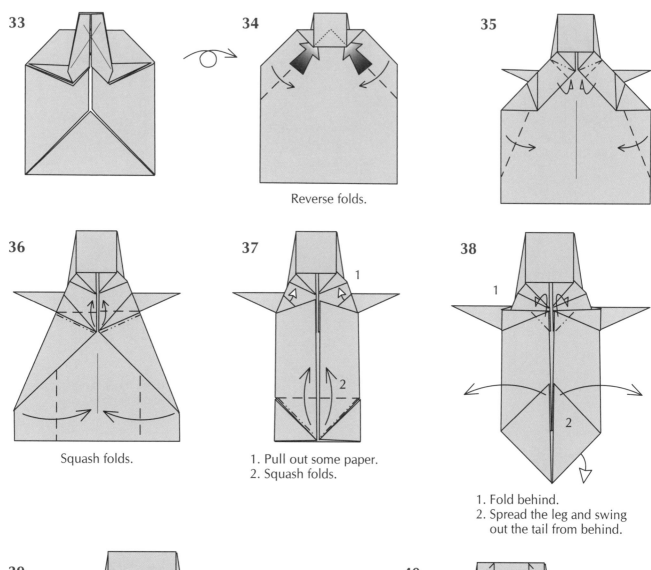

33

34

Reverse folds.

35

36

Squash folds.

37

1. Pull out some paper.
2. Squash folds.

38

1. Fold behind.
2. Spread the leg and swing
   out the tail from behind.

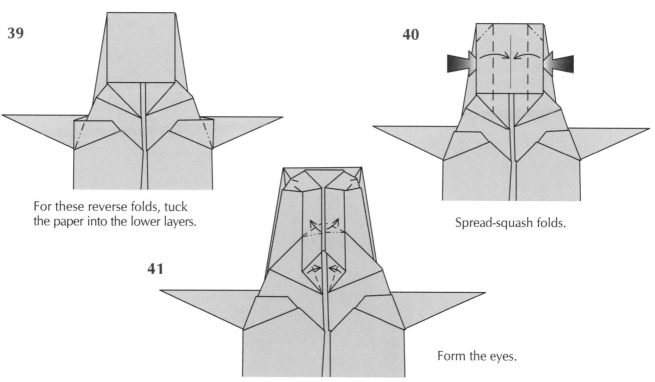

39

For these reverse folds, tuck
the paper into the lower layers.

40

Spread-squash folds.

41

Form the eyes.

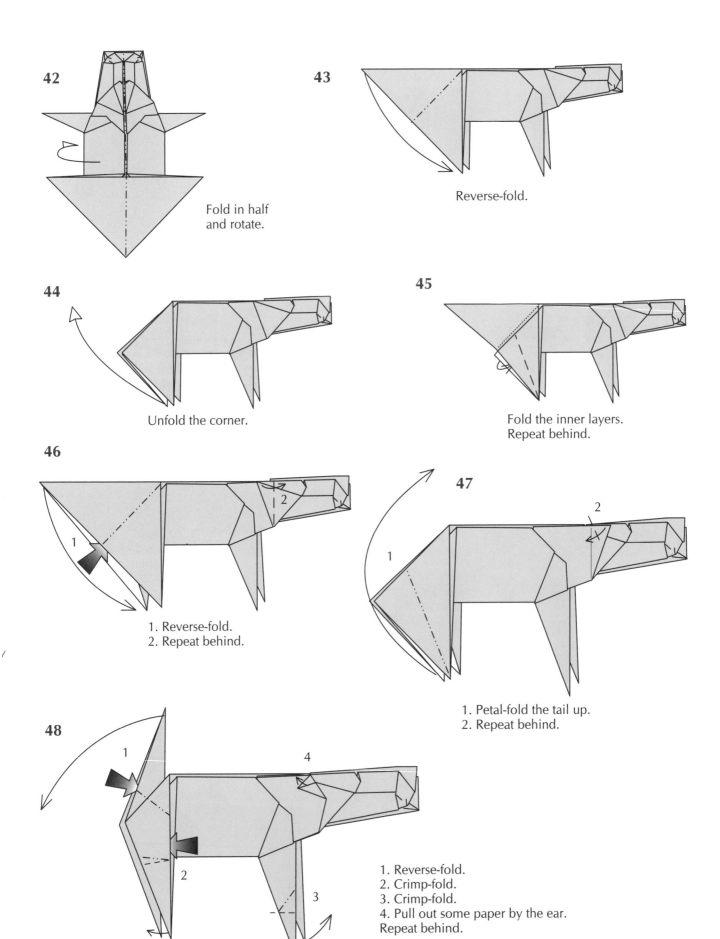

42

Fold in half
and rotate.

43

Reverse-fold.

44

Unfold the corner.

45

Fold the inner layers.
Repeat behind.

46

1
2

1. Reverse-fold.
2. Repeat behind.

47

1
2

1. Petal-fold the tail up.
2. Repeat behind.

48

1
2
3
4

1. Reverse-fold.
2. Crimp-fold.
3. Crimp-fold.
4. Pull out some paper by the ear.
Repeat behind.

49

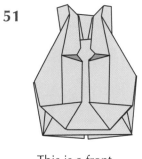

1. Thin the tail.
2. Shape the foot.
3. Reverse-fold.
Repeat behind.

50

1. Outside-reverse-fold.
2. Flatten the head, open the mouth, and shape the back. Repeat behind.

51

This is a front view of the head.

52

This is a view of the jaw. Rabbit-ear to form two teeth.

53

Tuck the corners under the teeth.

54

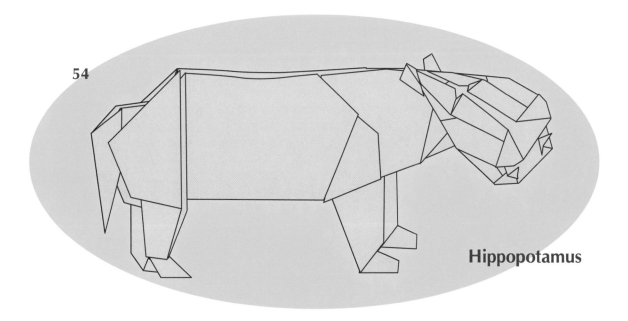

Hippopotamus

Kangaroo

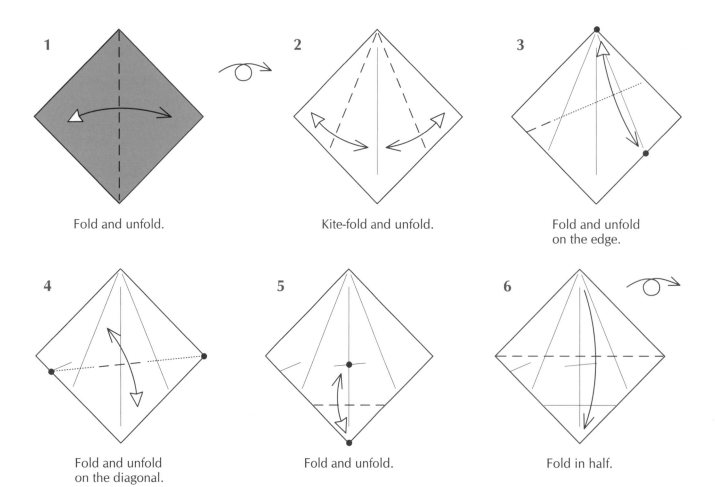

1 Fold and unfold.

2 Kite-fold and unfold.

3 Fold and unfold on the edge.

4 Fold and unfold on the diagonal.

5 Fold and unfold.

6 Fold in half.

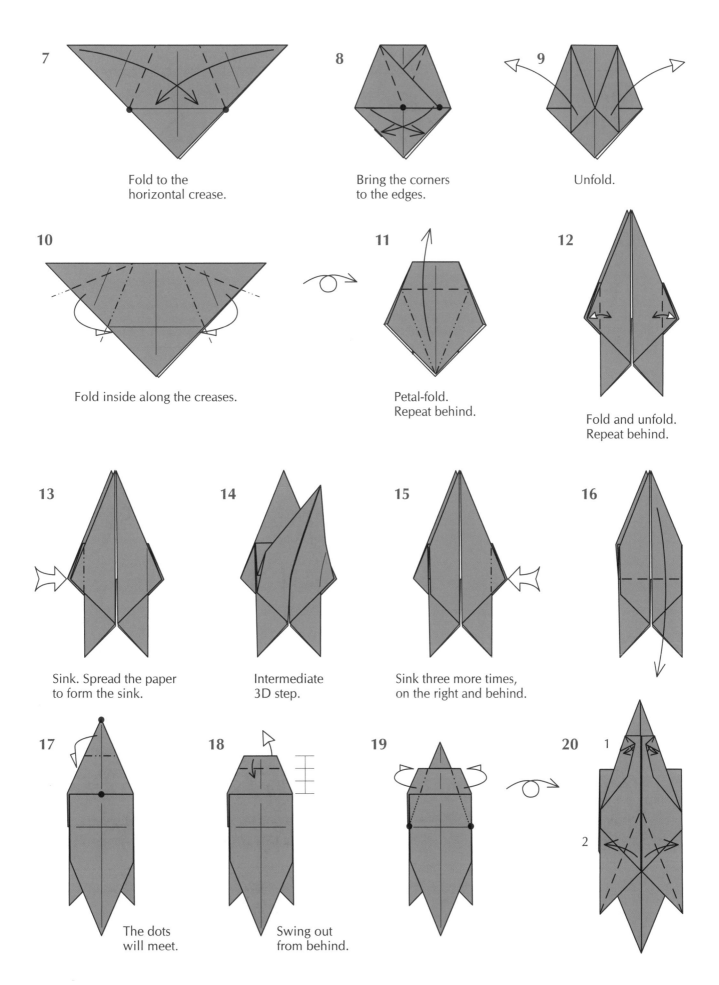

7 Fold to the horizontal crease.

8 Bring the corners to the edges.

9 Unfold.

10 Fold inside along the creases.

11 Petal-fold. Repeat behind.

12 Fold and unfold. Repeat behind.

13 Sink. Spread the paper to form the sink.

14 Intermediate 3D step.

15 Sink three more times, on the right and behind.

16

17 The dots will meet.

18 Swing out from behind.

19

20 1 2

21

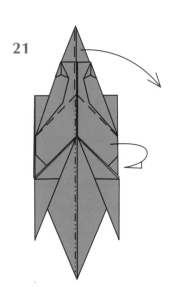

Lift the head while
folding in half. Rotate.

22

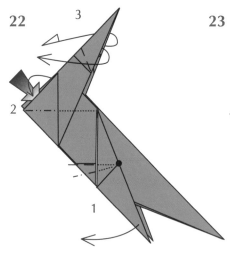

1. Pivot at the dot. Repeat behind.
2. Reverse-fold.
3. Outside-reverse-fold.

23

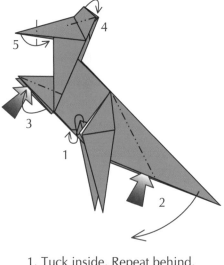

1. Tuck inside. Repeat behind.
2. Reverse-fold the tail.
3. Reverse-fold the inner layer.
4. Reverse-fold the ears.
5. Reverse-fold the head.

24

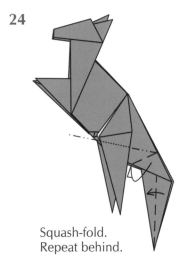

Squash-fold.
Repeat behind.

25

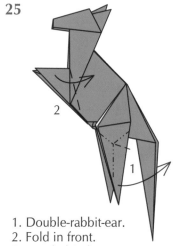

1. Double-rabbit-ear.
2. Fold in front.
Repeat behind.

26

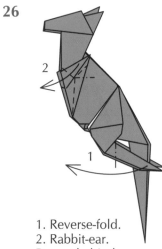

1. Reverse-fold.
2. Rabbit-ear.
Repeat behind.

27

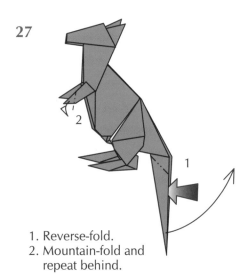

1. Reverse-fold.
2. Mountain-fold and
repeat behind.

28

Kangaroo

Lion

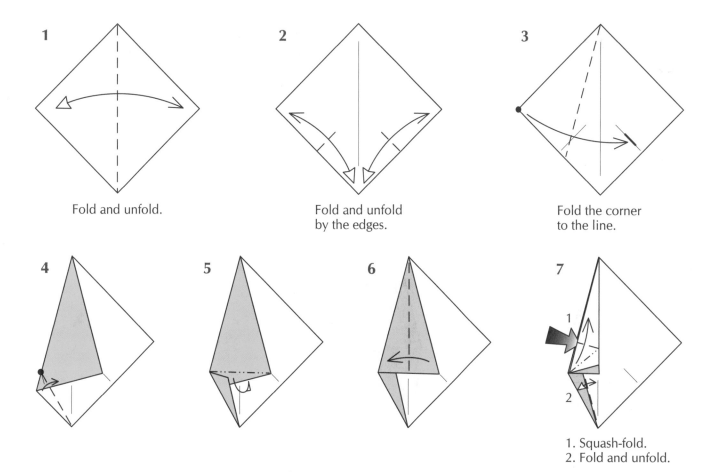

1

Fold and unfold.

2

Fold and unfold by the edges.

3

Fold the corner to the line.

4

5

6

7

1. Squash-fold.
2. Fold and unfold.

8

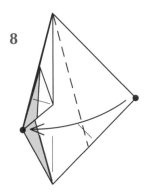

Repeat steps 3–7
on the right.

9

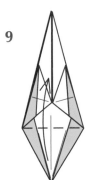

10

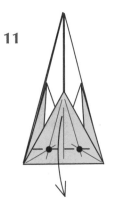

Fold and unfold
the top layers.

11

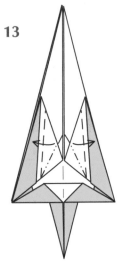

12

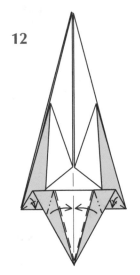

Squash folds.

13

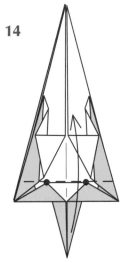

Spread-squash folds.

14

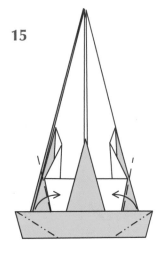

15

This is similar to
a reverse fold.

16

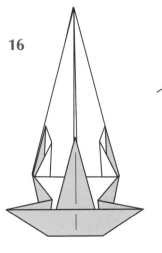

17

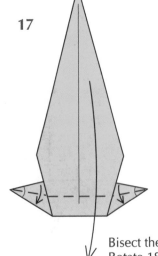

Bisect the angles.
Rotate 180°.

18

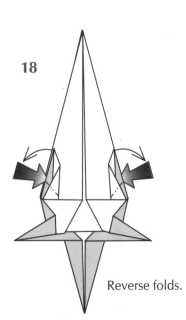

Reverse folds.

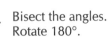

19

20

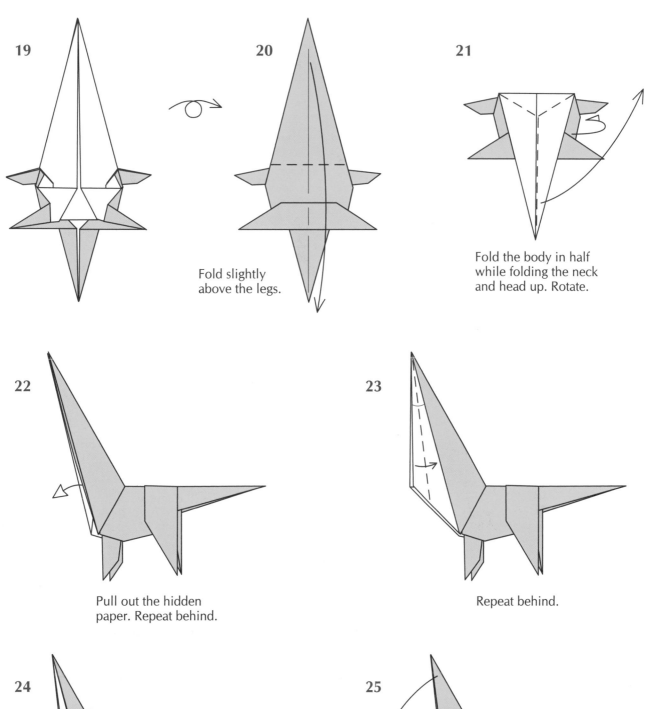

Fold slightly
above the legs.

21

Fold the body in half
while folding the neck
and head up. Rotate.

22

Pull out the hidden
paper. Repeat behind.

23

Repeat behind.

24

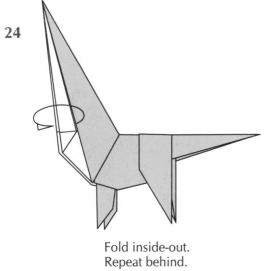

Fold inside-out.
Repeat behind.

25

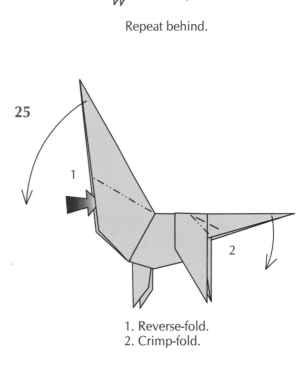

1

2

1. Reverse-fold.
2. Crimp-fold.

26

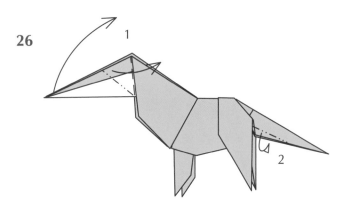

1. Crimp-fold.
2. Fold inside and repeat behind.

27

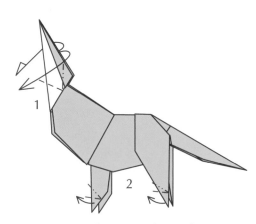

1. Combination of outside reverse and squash folds.
2. Crimp folds.
Repeat behind.

28

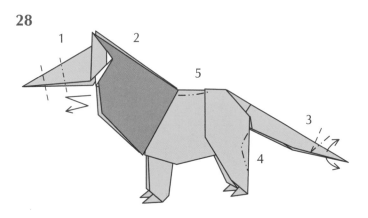

1. Reverse folds.
2. Bring the dark paper to the front.
3. Spread the tail.
4. Shape the legs.
5. Shape the back.
Repeat behind.

29

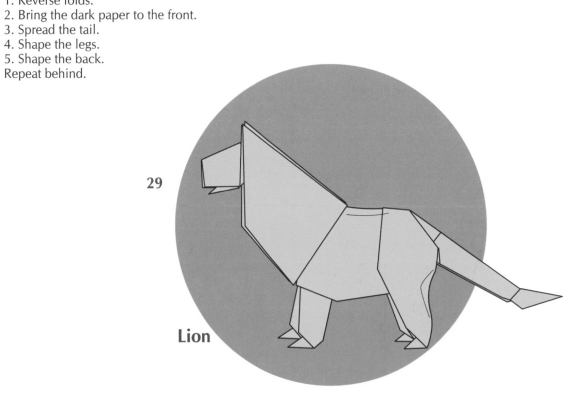

Lion

Moose

1

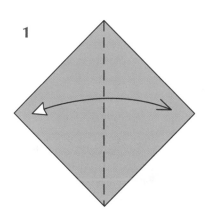

Fold and unfold.

2

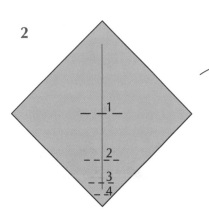

Fold and unfold
in half four times.

3

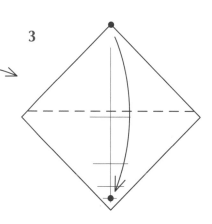

4

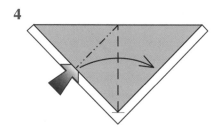

Squash-fold.

5

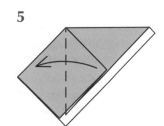

6

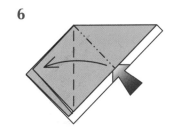

Repeat steps 4–5
on the right.

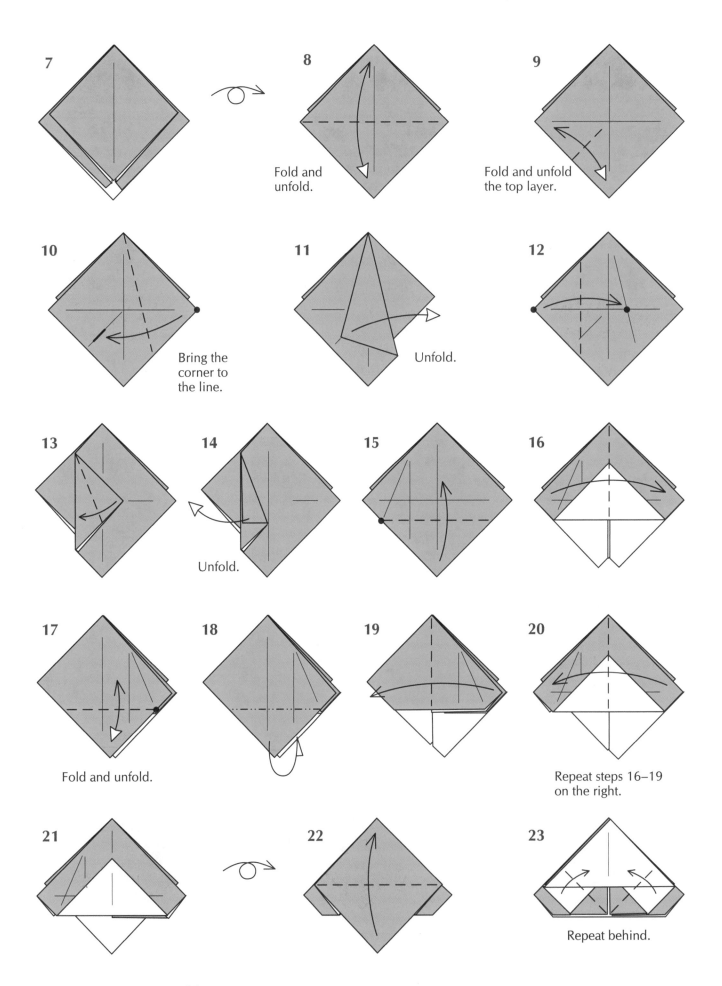

7

8
Fold and unfold.

9
Fold and unfold the top layer.

10
Bring the corner to the line.

11
Unfold.

12

13

14
Unfold.

15

16

17
Fold and unfold.

18

19

20
Repeat steps 16–19 on the right.

21

22

23
Repeat behind.

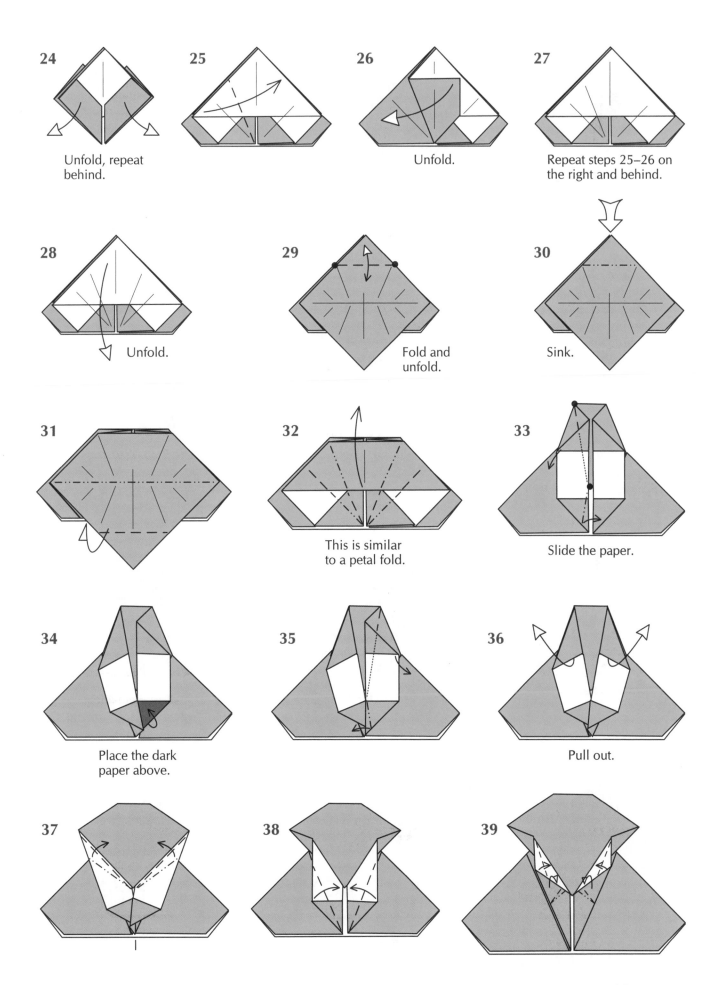

24 Unfold, repeat behind.

25

26 Unfold.

27 Repeat steps 25–26 on the right and behind.

28 Unfold.

29 Fold and unfold.

30 Sink.

31

32 This is similar to a petal fold.

33 Slide the paper.

34 Place the dark paper above.

35

36 Pull out.

37

38

39

40

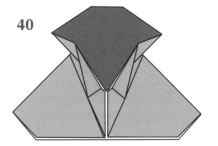

Bring the dark
paper to the front.

41

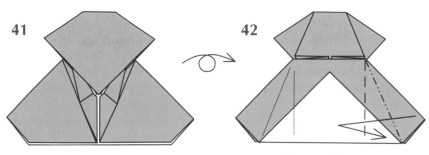

42

Fold along the creases.

43

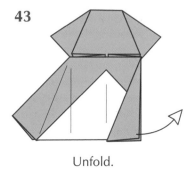

Unfold.

44

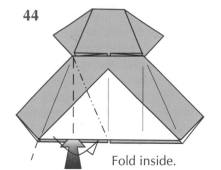

Fold inside.

45

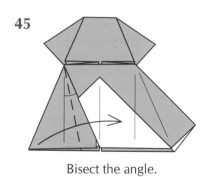

Bisect the angle.

46

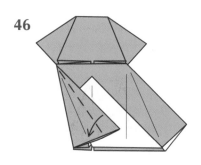

47

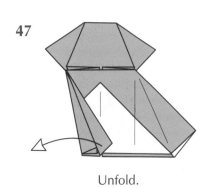

Unfold.

48

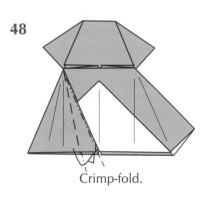

Crimp-fold.

49

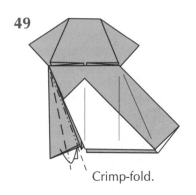

Crimp-fold.

50

Reverse-fold.

51

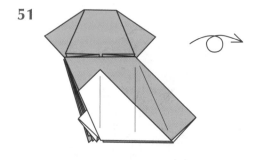

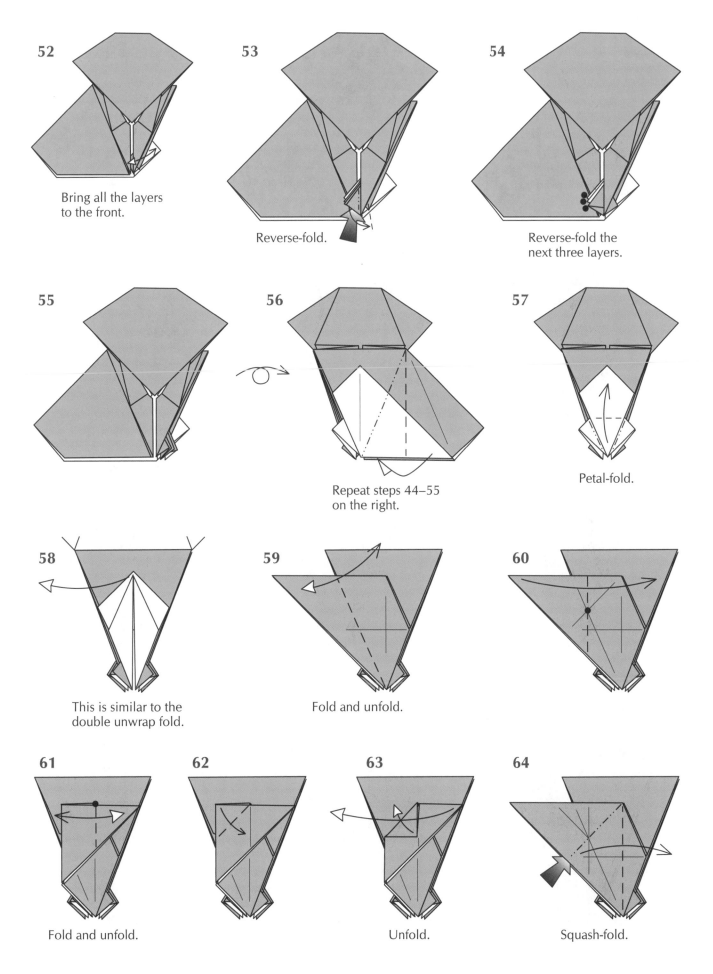

52

Bring all the layers to the front.

53

Reverse-fold.

54

Reverse-fold the next three layers.

55

56

Repeat steps 44–55 on the right.

57

Petal-fold.

58

This is similar to the double unwrap fold.

59

Fold and unfold.

60

61

Fold and unfold.

62

63

Unfold.

64

Squash-fold.

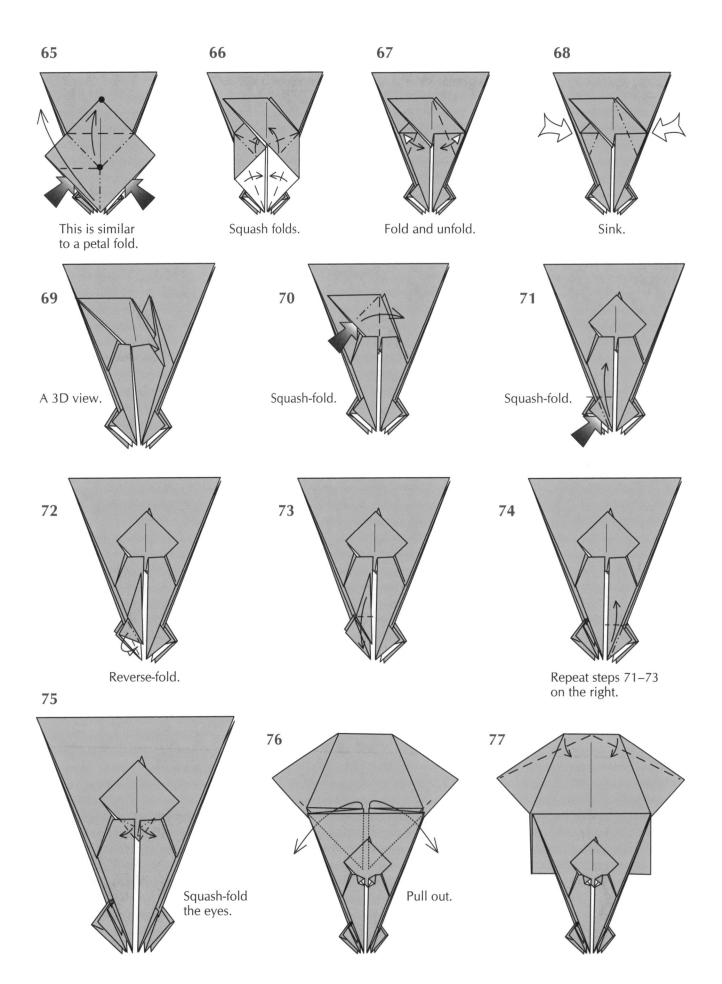

65

This is similar
to a petal fold.

66

Squash folds.

67

Fold and unfold.

68

Sink.

69

A 3D view.

70

Squash-fold.

71

Squash-fold.

72

Reverse-fold.

73

74

Repeat steps 71–73
on the right.

75

Squash-fold
the eyes.

76

Pull out.

77

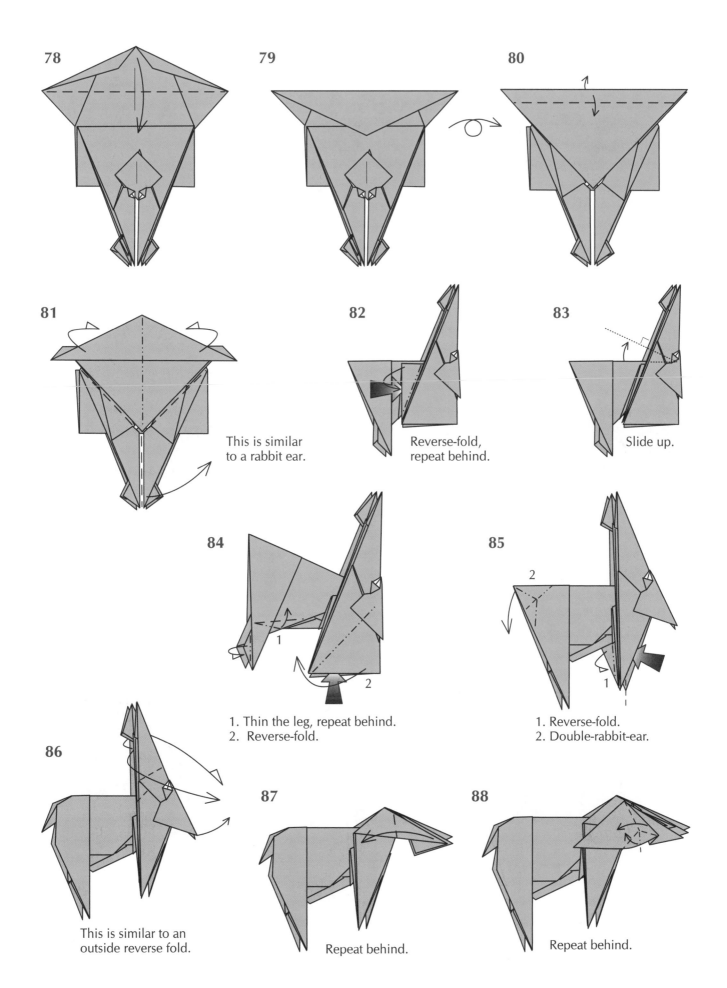

78

79

80

81

This is similar to a rabbit ear.

82

Reverse-fold, repeat behind.

83

Slide up.

84

1. Thin the leg, repeat behind.
2. Reverse-fold.

85

1. Reverse-fold.
2. Double-rabbit-ear.

86

This is similar to an outside reverse fold.

87

Repeat behind.

88

Repeat behind.

Moose 91

89

Repeat behind.

90

Repeat behind.

91

Repeat behind.

92

Thin the legs and shape
the head. Repeat behind.

93

Repeat behind.

94

Moose

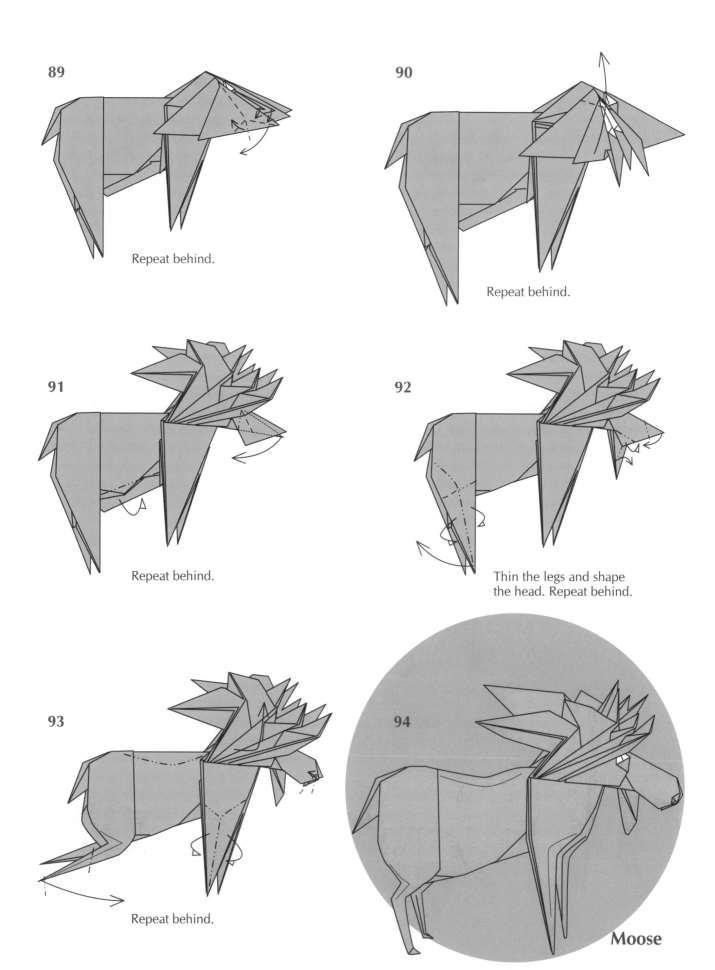

Panda

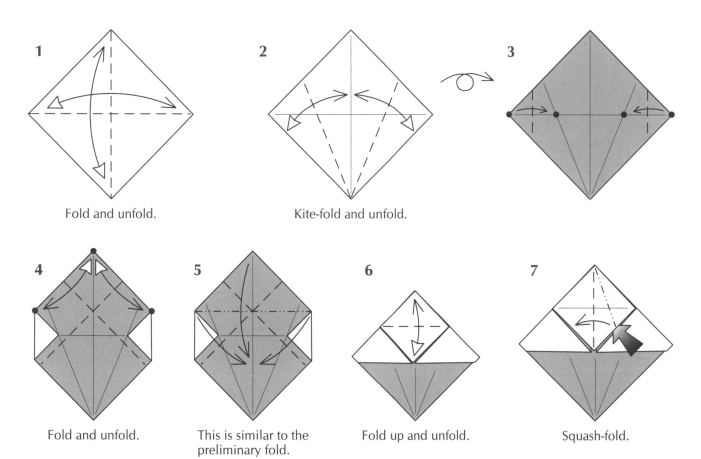

1

Fold and unfold.

2

Kite-fold and unfold.

3

4

Fold and unfold.

5

This is similar to the preliminary fold.

6

Fold up and unfold.

7

Squash-fold.

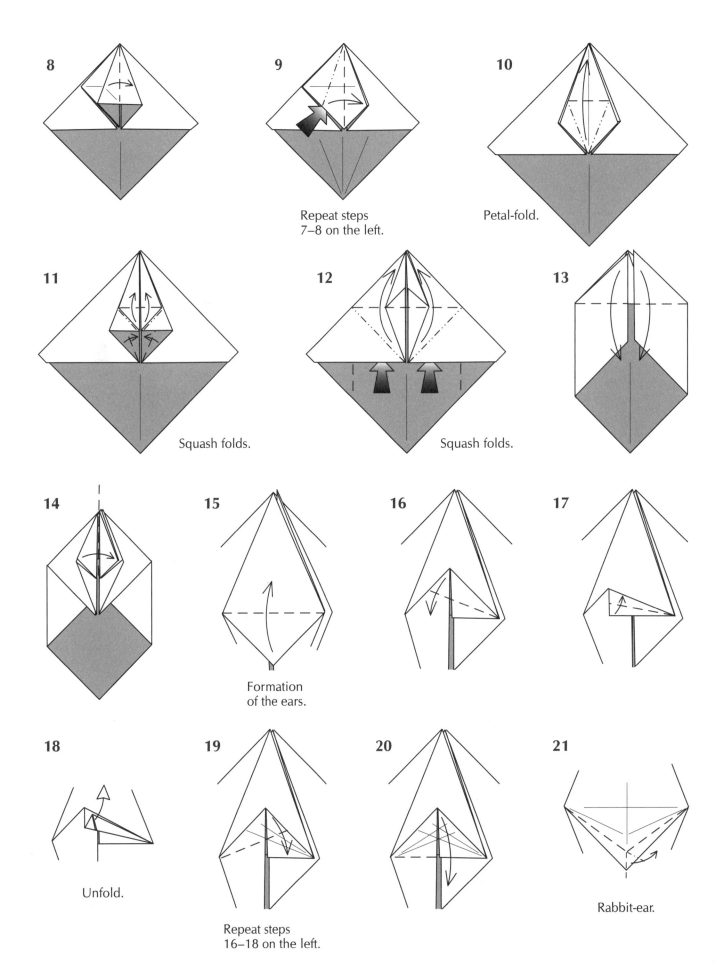

8

9

Repeat steps
7–8 on the left.

10

Petal-fold.

11

Squash folds.

12

Squash folds.

13

14

15

Formation
of the ears.

16

17

18

Unfold.

19

Repeat steps
16–18 on the left.

20

21

Rabbit-ear.

22

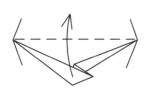

23

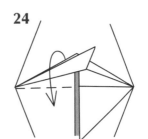

This is similar
to a rabbit ear.

24

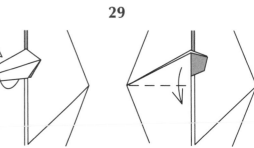

25

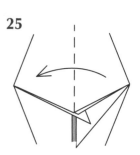

26

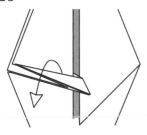

Unlock some paper.

27

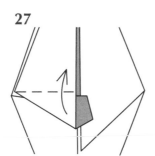

28

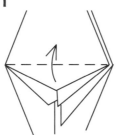

Unlock some paper.

29

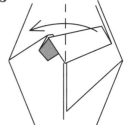

30

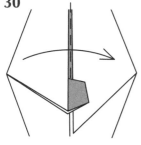

31

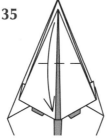

32

Squash-fold. Note
the right angle.

33

34

Repeat steps 14–33
on the right.

35

Unfold.

36

37

Note the
right angle.

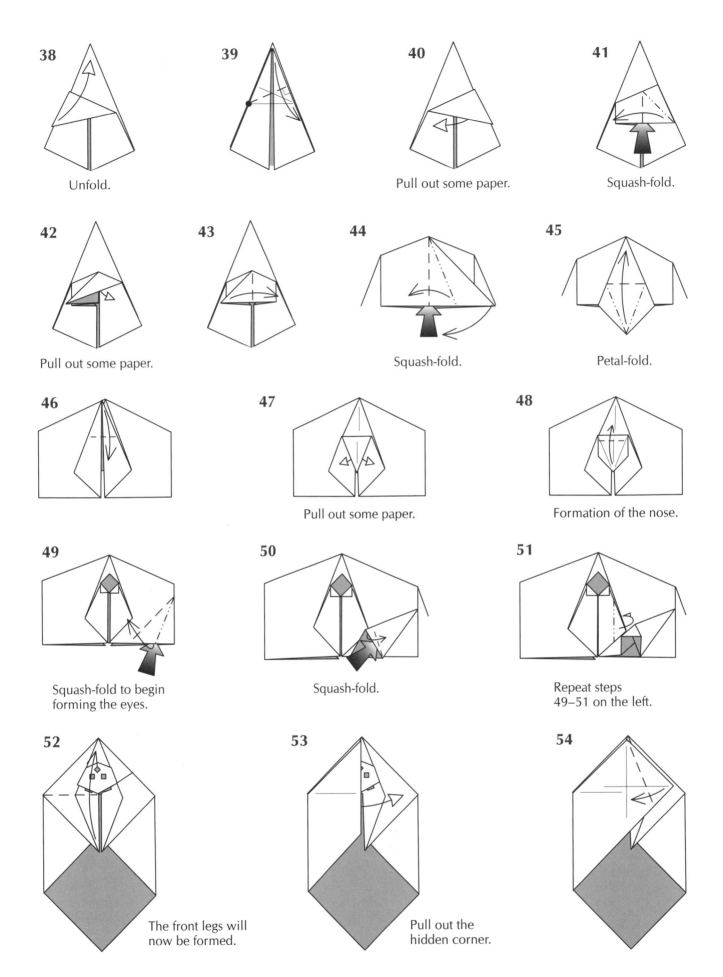

38

Unfold.

39

40

Pull out some paper.

41

Squash-fold.

42

Pull out some paper.

43

44

Squash-fold.

45

Petal-fold.

46

47

Pull out some paper.

48

Formation of the nose.

49

Squash-fold to begin forming the eyes.

50

Squash-fold.

51

Repeat steps 49–51 on the left.

52

The front legs will now be formed.

53

Pull out the hidden corner.

54

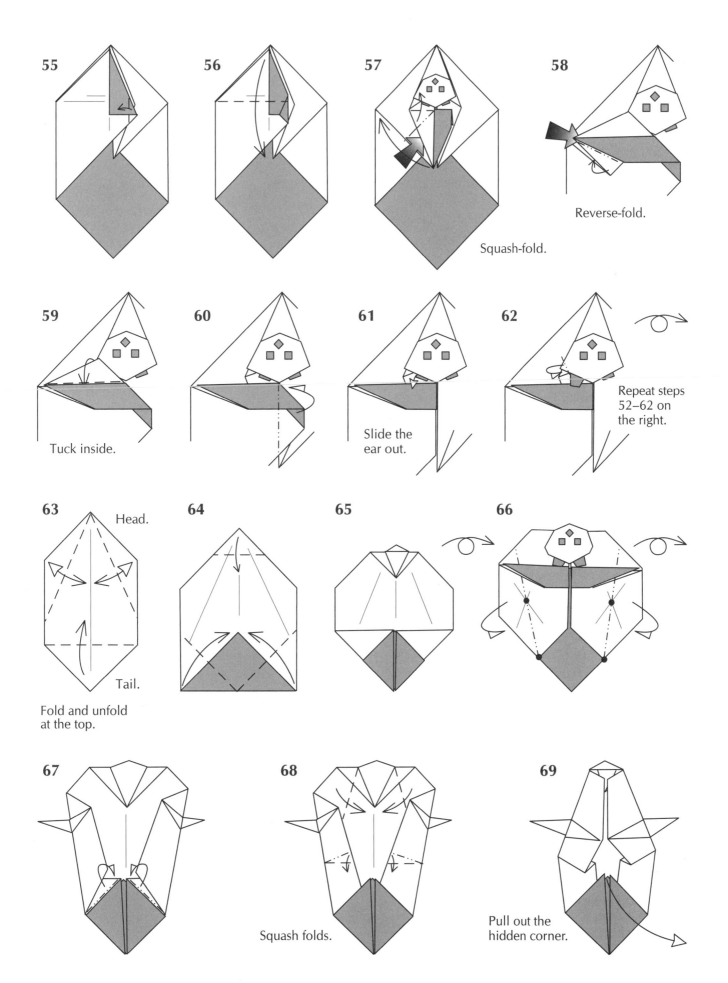

55

56

57

Squash-fold.

58

Reverse-fold.

59

Tuck inside.

60

61

Slide the
ear out.

62

Repeat steps
52–62 on
the right.

63

Head.

Tail.

Fold and unfold
at the top.

64

65

66

67

68

Squash folds.

69

Pull out the
hidden corner.

70

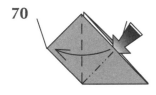

Squash-fold.

71

Tail.

72

73

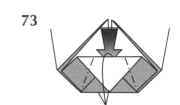

Petal-fold.

74

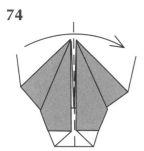

75

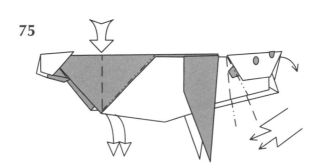

Fold the back legs down
and crimp fold the neck.

76

Repeat behind.

77

Reverse-fold.

78

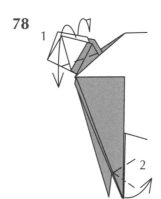

1. Outside-reverse-fold the tail.
2. Pull some paper out to form
the foot. Repeat behind.

79

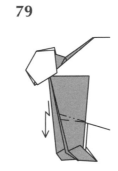

Crimp-fold,
repeat behind.

80

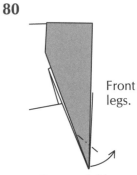

Front
legs.

Reverse-fold,
repeat behind.

81

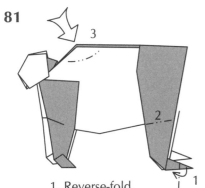

1. Reverse-fold.
2. Bend at the knee.
3. Shape the back.
Repeat behind.

82

Panda

Rabbit

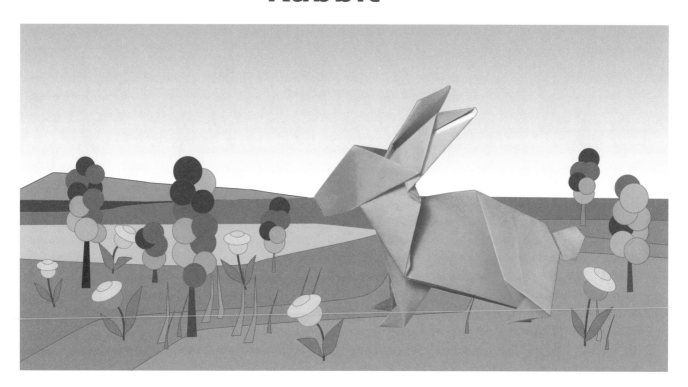

1

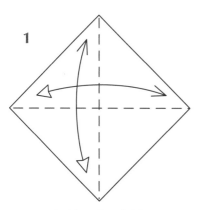

Fold and unfold.

2

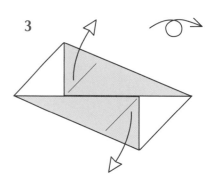

Fold to the center.

3

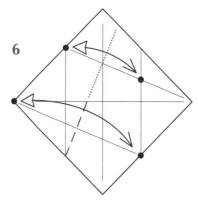

Unfold.

4

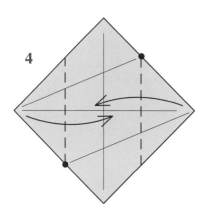

5

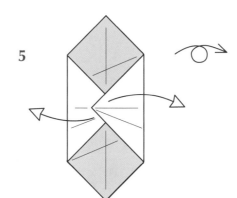

Unfold.

6

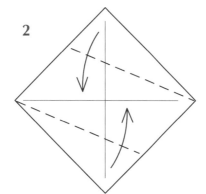

Fold and unfold on the bottom half so the pairs of dots meet.

7

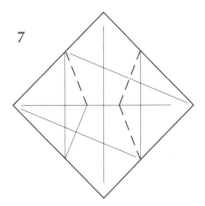

Repeat step 6
three more times.

8

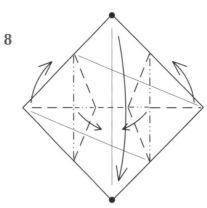

Collapse along the
creases so the dots meet.

9

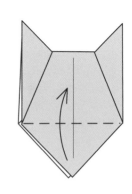

10

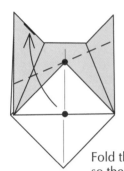

Fold the top layers up
so the lower dot meets
the bold edge.

11

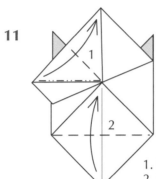

1. Squash-fold.
2. Fold up.

12

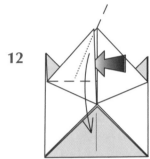

Squash-fold.

13

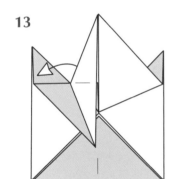

Pull out.

14

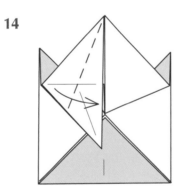

15

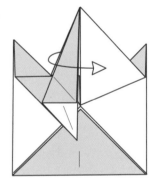

Unfold.

16

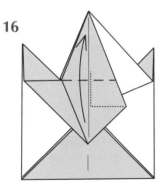

Squash-fold.

17

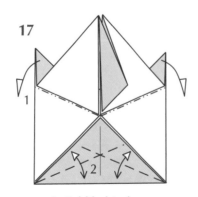

1. Fold behind.
2. Fold and unfold
   the top layer.

18

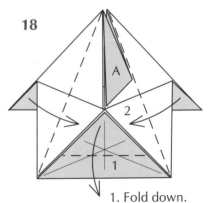

1. Fold down.
2. Fold under A
   on the right.

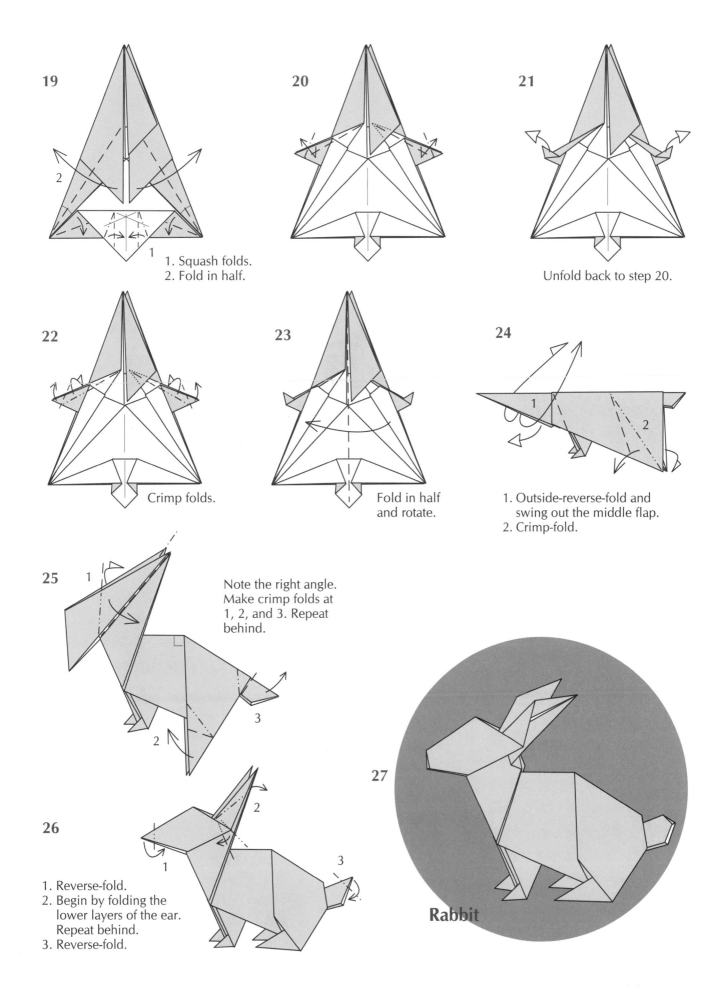

19

1. Squash folds.
2. Fold in half.

20

21

Unfold back to step 20.

22

Crimp folds.

23

Fold in half
and rotate.

24

1. Outside-reverse-fold and
   swing out the middle flap.
2. Crimp-fold.

25

Note the right angle.
Make crimp folds at
1, 2, and 3. Repeat
behind.

26

1. Reverse-fold.
2. Begin by folding the
   lower layers of the ear.
   Repeat behind.
3. Reverse-fold.

27

Rabbit

Raccoon

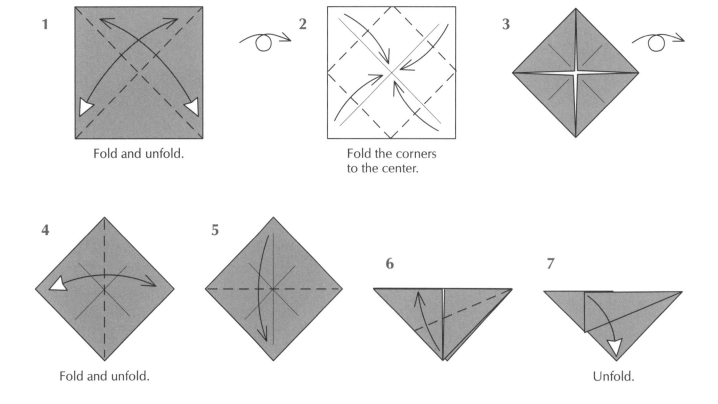

1 Fold and unfold.

2 Fold the corners to the center.

3

4 Fold and unfold.

5

6

7 Unfold.

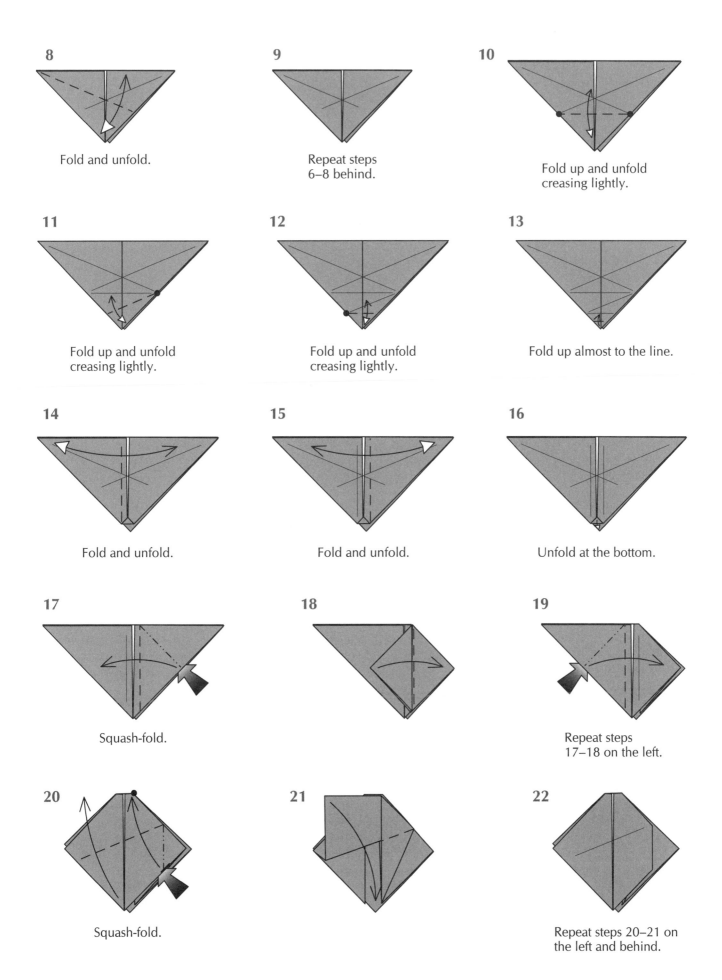

8

Fold and unfold.

9

Repeat steps
6–8 behind.

10

Fold up and unfold
creasing lightly.

11

Fold up and unfold
creasing lightly.

12

Fold up and unfold
creasing lightly.

13

Fold up almost to the line.

14

Fold and unfold.

15

Fold and unfold.

16

Unfold at the bottom.

17

Squash-fold.

18

19

Repeat steps
17–18 on the left.

20

Squash-fold.

21

22

Repeat steps 20–21 on
the left and behind.

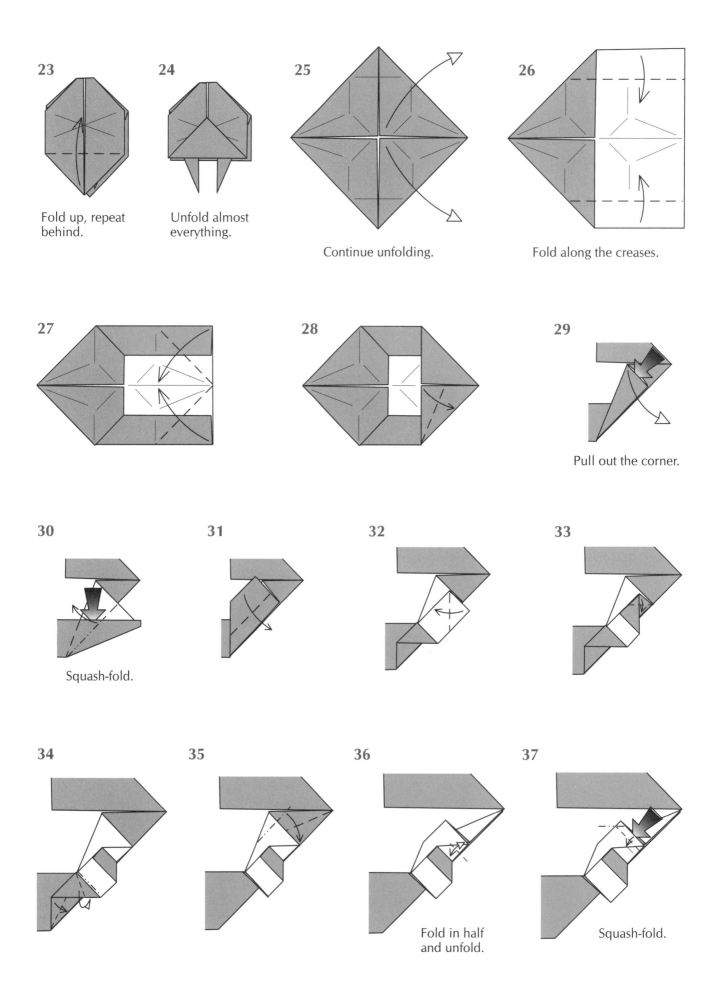

23 Fold up, repeat behind.

24 Unfold almost everything.

25 Continue unfolding.

26 Fold along the creases.

27

28

29 Pull out the corner.

30 Squash-fold.

31

32

33

34

35

36 Fold in half and unfold.

37 Squash-fold.

38

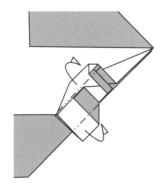

39

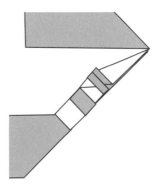

Repeat steps 28–38
on the top.

40

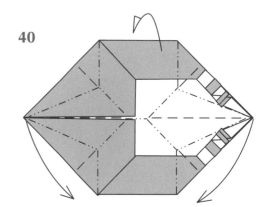

Collapse along the creases.

41

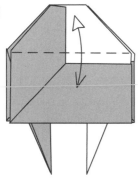

Fold and unfold.

42

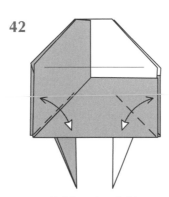

Fold and unfold.

43

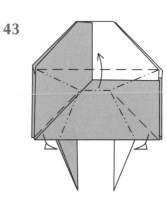

Fold the top layers along
several of the creases.

44

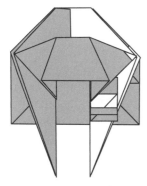

Repeat steps 41–43 behind.

45

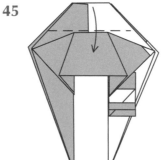

46

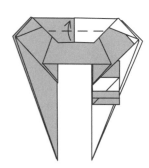

47

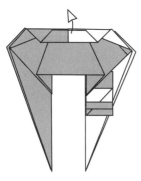

Unfold.

48

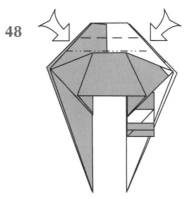

Sink down and up.

49

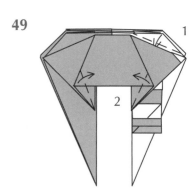

Tuck inside at 1.
Repeat behind.

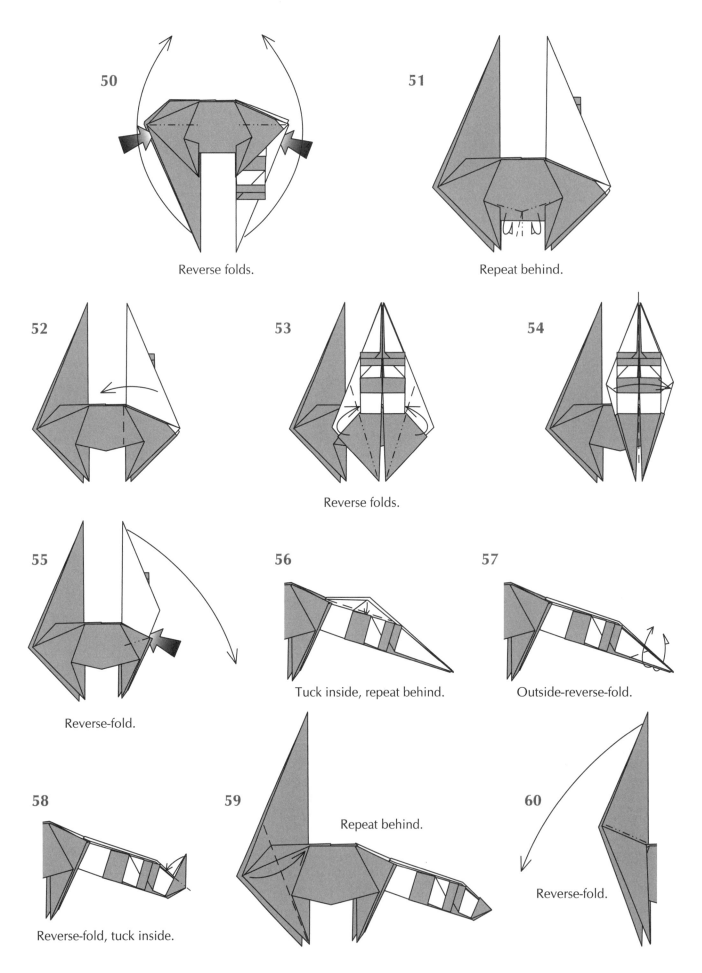

50

Reverse folds.

51

Repeat behind.

52

53

Reverse folds.

54

55

Reverse-fold.

56

Tuck inside, repeat behind.

57

Outside-reverse-fold.

58

Reverse-fold, tuck inside.

59

Repeat behind.

60

Reverse-fold.

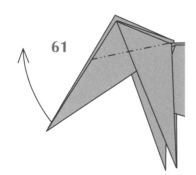

61

Reverse-fold.

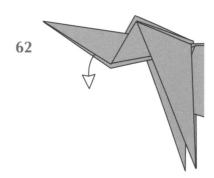

62

Pull out, repeat behind.

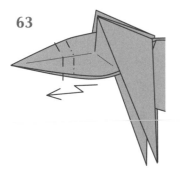

63

The head is 3D. Reverse folds.

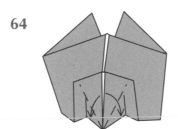

64

Front view.

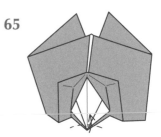

65

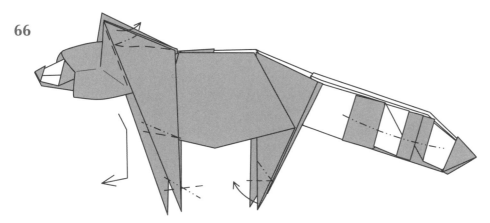

66

Shape the ears, legs, and tail. Repeat behind.

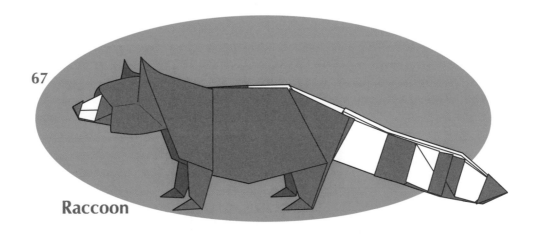

67

Raccoon

Rhinoceros

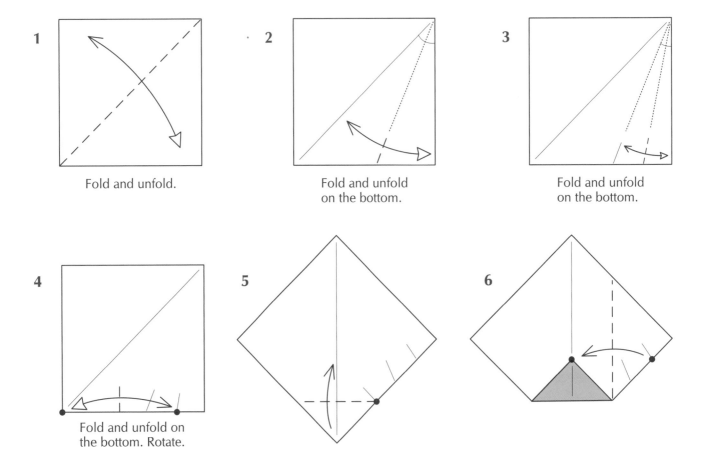

1 Fold and unfold.

2 Fold and unfold on the bottom.

3 Fold and unfold on the bottom.

4 Fold and unfold on the bottom. Rotate.

5

6

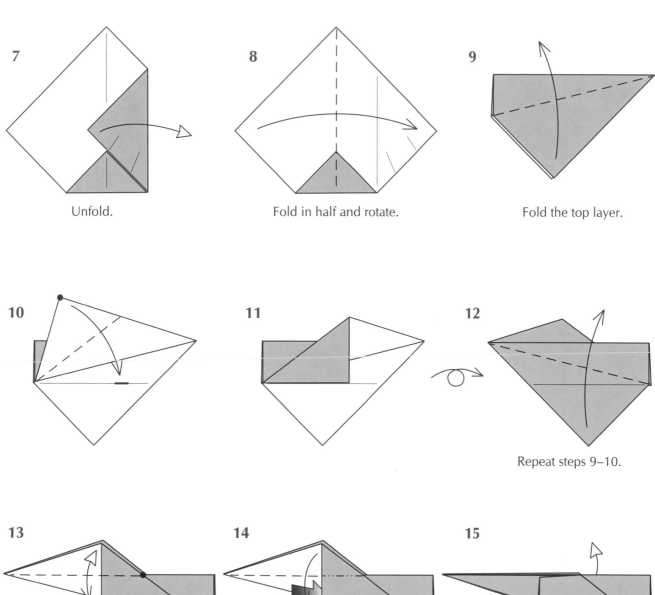

7

Unfold.

8

Fold in half and rotate.

9

Fold the top layer.

10

11

12

Repeat steps 9–10.

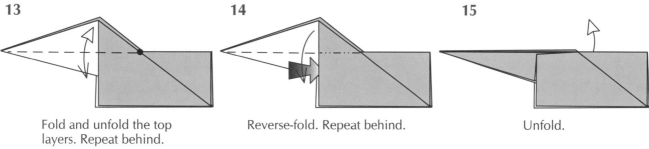

13

Fold and unfold the top layers. Repeat behind.

14

Reverse-fold. Repeat behind.

15

Unfold.

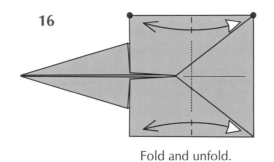

16

Fold and unfold.

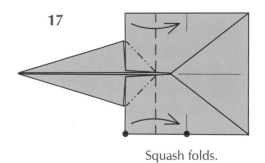

17

Squash folds.

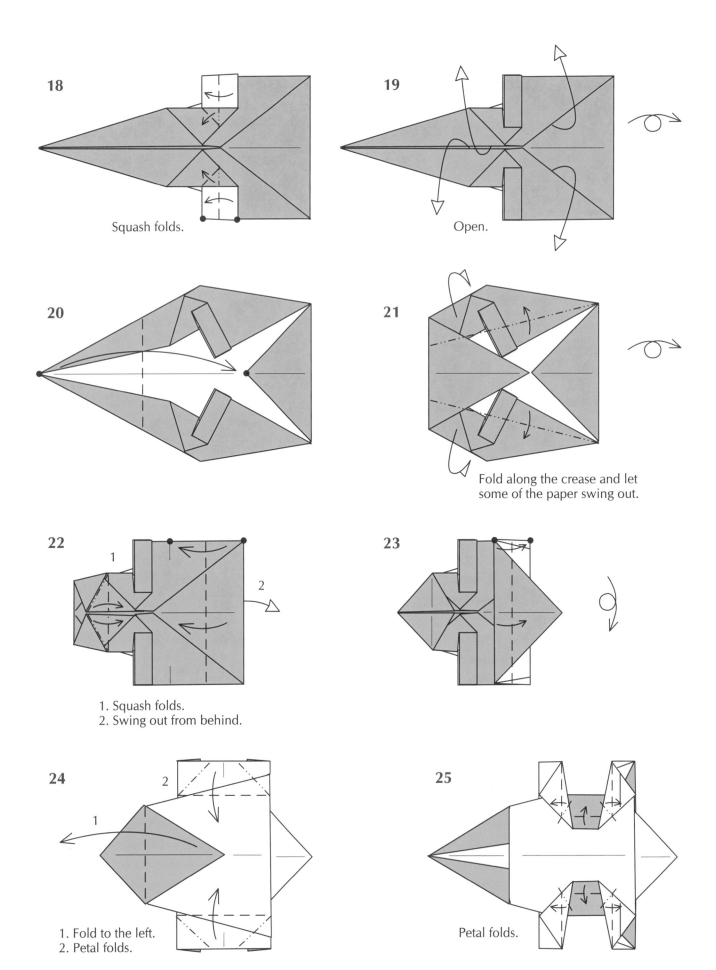

18

Squash folds.

19

Open.

20

21

Fold along the crease and let
some of the paper swing out.

22

1. Squash folds.
2. Swing out from behind.

23

24

1. Fold to the left.
2. Petal folds.

25

Petal folds.

26

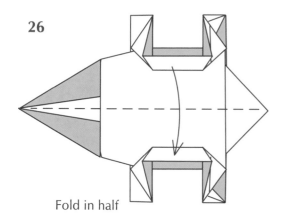

Fold in half

27

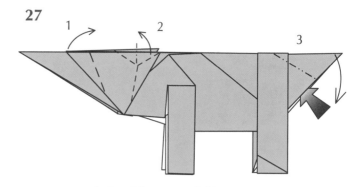

1. Outside-reverse-fold.
2. Rabbit-ear and repeat behind.
3. Reverse-fold.

28

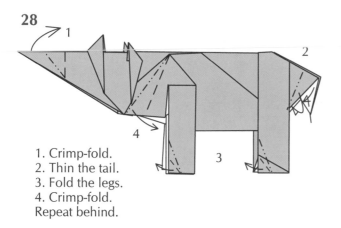

1. Crimp-fold.
2. Thin the tail.
3. Fold the legs.
4. Crimp-fold.
Repeat behind.

29

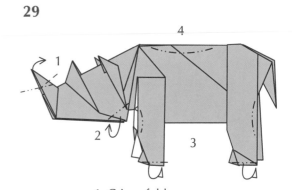

1. Crimp-fold.
2. Reverse-fold.
3. Shape the legs.
4. Shape the back.
Repeat behind.

30

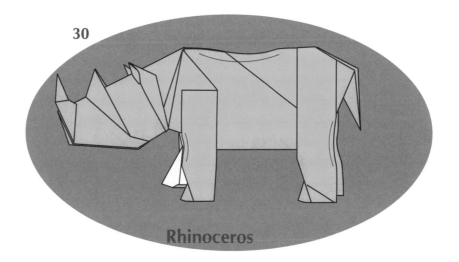

Rhinoceros

Squirrel

1

Fold and unfold.

2

Fold and unfold.

3

Make the preliminary fold.

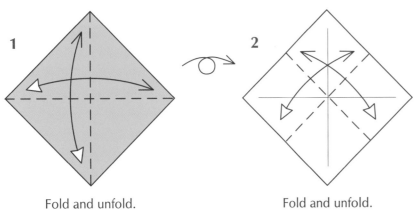

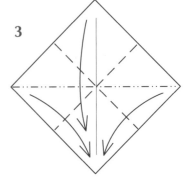

4

Kite-fold, repeat behind.

5

Unfold, repeat behind.

6

Petal-fold, repeat behind.

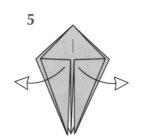

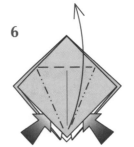

7

Rabbit-ear.

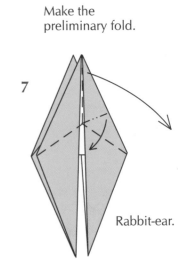

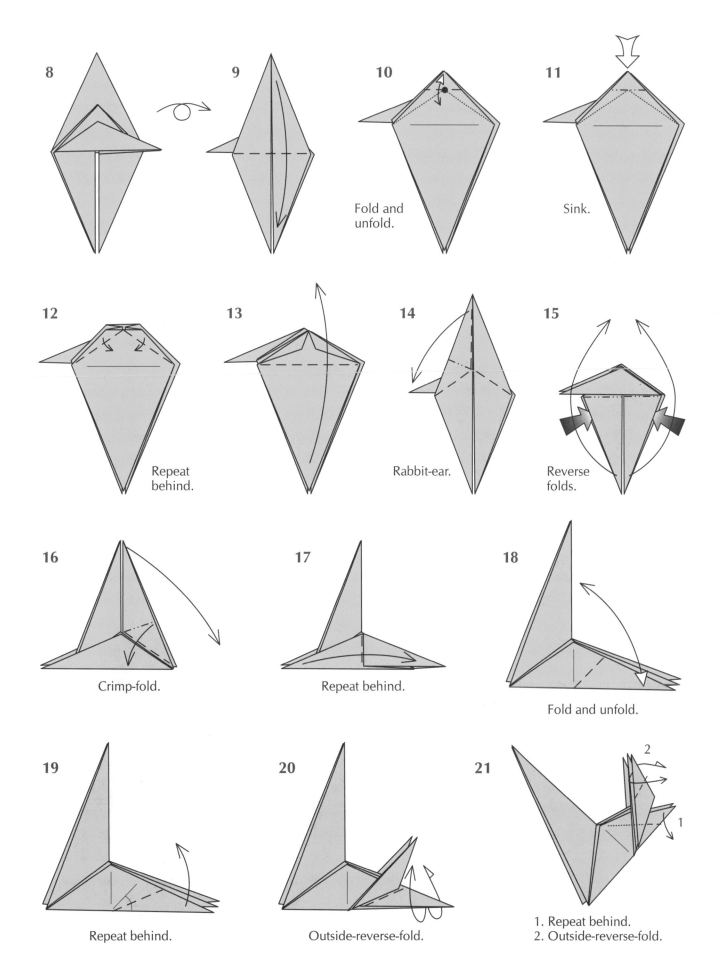

8

9

10 Fold and unfold.

11 Sink.

12 Repeat behind.

13

14 Rabbit-ear.

15 Reverse folds.

16 Crimp-fold.

17 Repeat behind.

18 Fold and unfold.

19 Repeat behind.

20 Outside-reverse-fold.

21
1. Repeat behind.
2. Outside-reverse-fold.

Squirrel 113

22

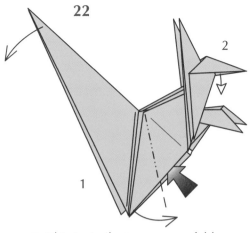

1. This is similar to a reverse-fold, repeat behind at the same time.
2. Pull out, repeat behind.

23

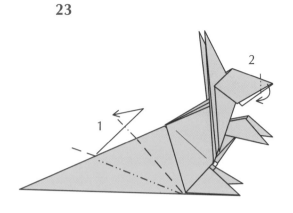

1. Crimp-fold.
2. Reverse-fold.

24

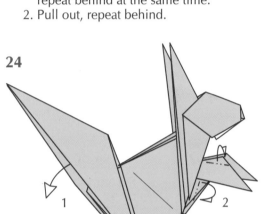

1. Pull out.
2. Thin the arms.
Repeat behind.

25

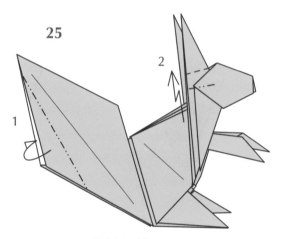

1. Fold inside.
2. Crimp-fold the ears.
Repeat behind.

26

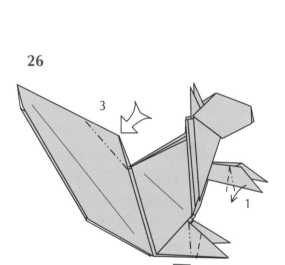

1. Squash-fold.
2. Crimp-fold.
3. Sink.
Repeat behind.

27

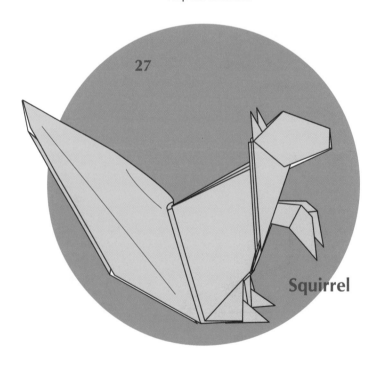

Squirrel

Turtle

1

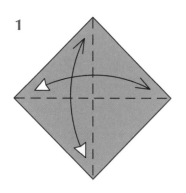

Fold and unfold.

2

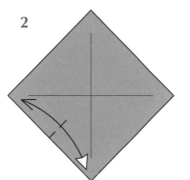

Fold and unfold
on the edge.

3

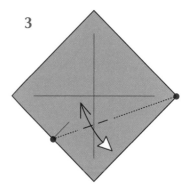

Fold and unfold
on the diagonal.

4

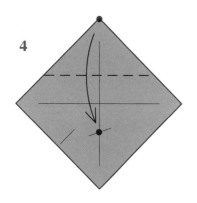

5

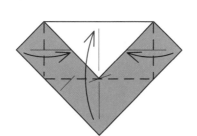

6

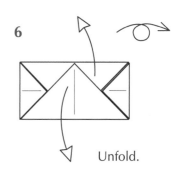

Unfold.

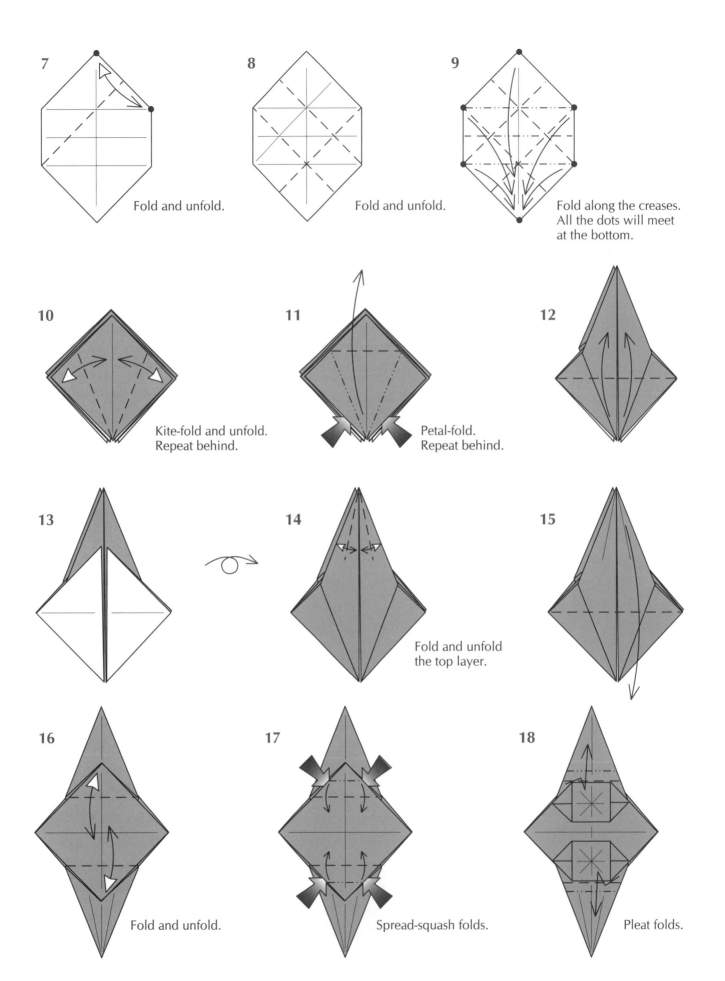

7 Fold and unfold.

8 Fold and unfold.

9 Fold along the creases. All the dots will meet at the bottom.

10 Kite-fold and unfold. Repeat behind.

11 Petal-fold. Repeat behind.

12

13

14 Fold and unfold the top layer.

15

16 Fold and unfold.

17 Spread-squash folds.

18 Pleat folds.

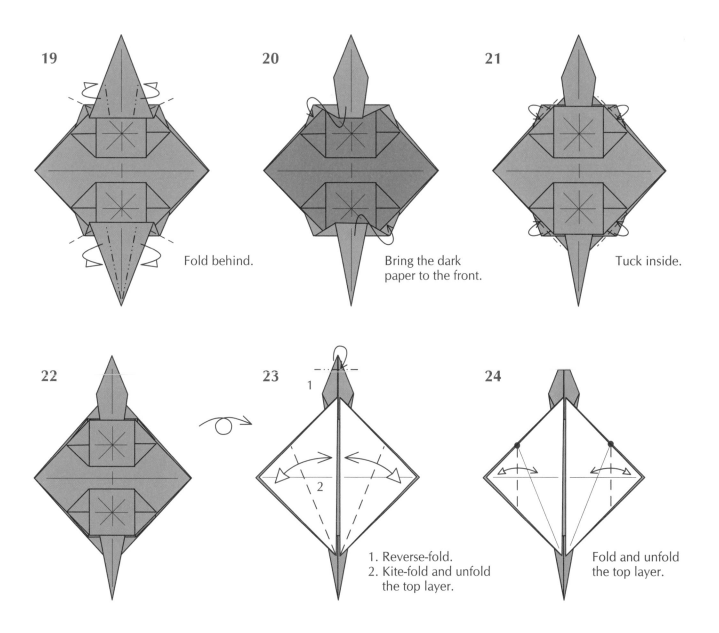

19

Fold behind.

20

Bring the dark
paper to the front.

21

Tuck inside.

22

23

1. Reverse-fold.
2. Kite-fold and unfold
   the top layer.

24

Fold and unfold
the top layer.

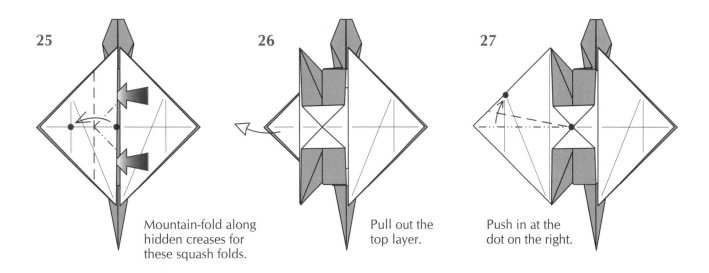

25

Mountain-fold along
hidden creases for
these squash folds.

26

Pull out the
top layer.

27

Push in at the
dot on the right.

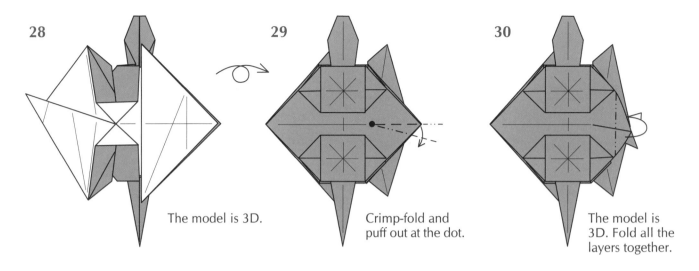

28

The model is 3D.

29

Crimp-fold and puff out at the dot.

30

The model is 3D. Fold all the layers together.

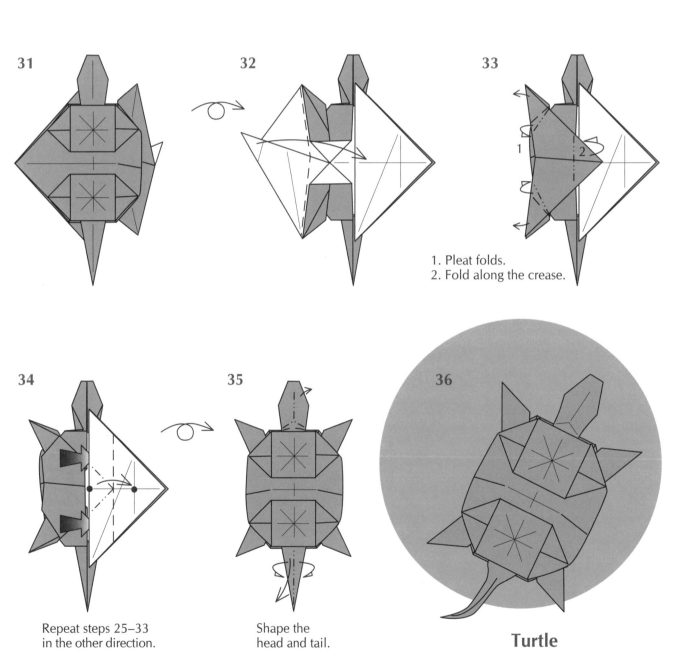

31

32

33

1. Pleat folds.
2. Fold along the crease.

34

Repeat steps 25–33 in the other direction.

35

Shape the head and tail.

36

Turtle

Zebra

This model was inspired by my
friend, Fumiaki Kawahata-san.

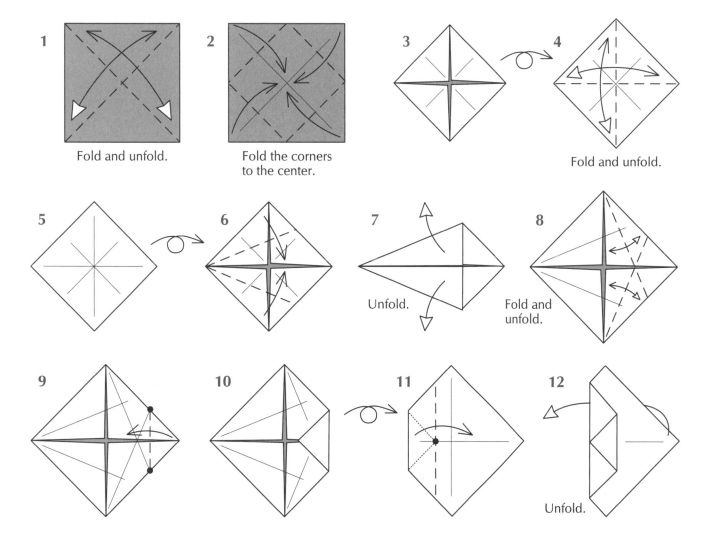

1 Fold and unfold.

2 Fold the corners
to the center.

3

4 Fold and unfold.

5

6

7 Unfold.

8 Fold and
unfold.

9

10

11

12 Unfold.

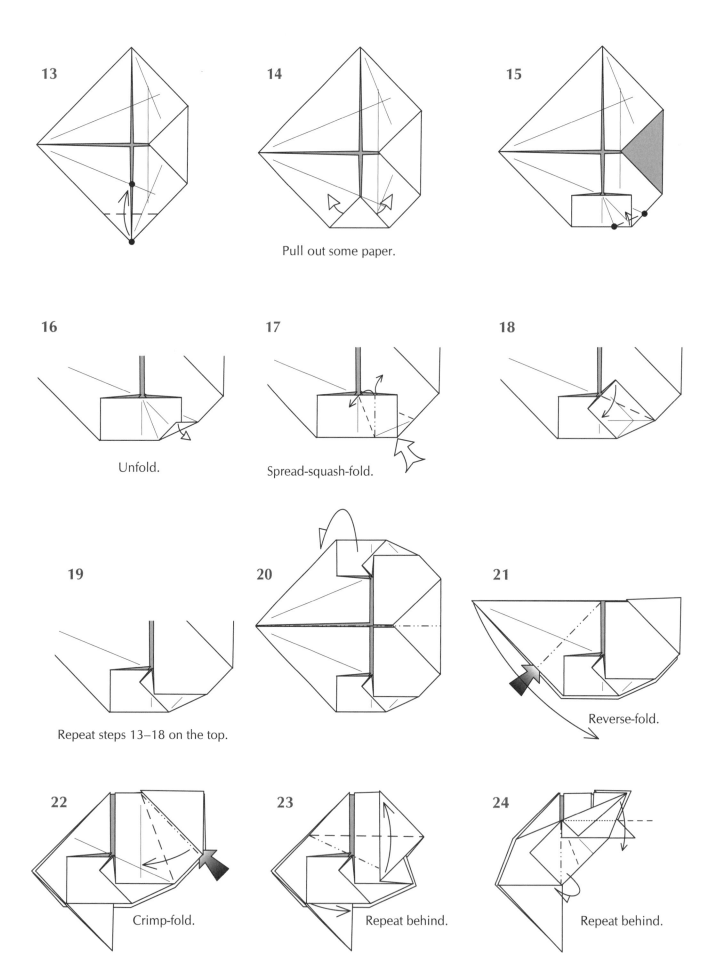

13

14

Pull out some paper.

15

16

Unfold.

17

Spread-squash-fold.

18

19

Repeat steps 13–18 on the top.

20

21

Reverse-fold.

22

Crimp-fold.

23

Repeat behind.

24

Repeat behind.

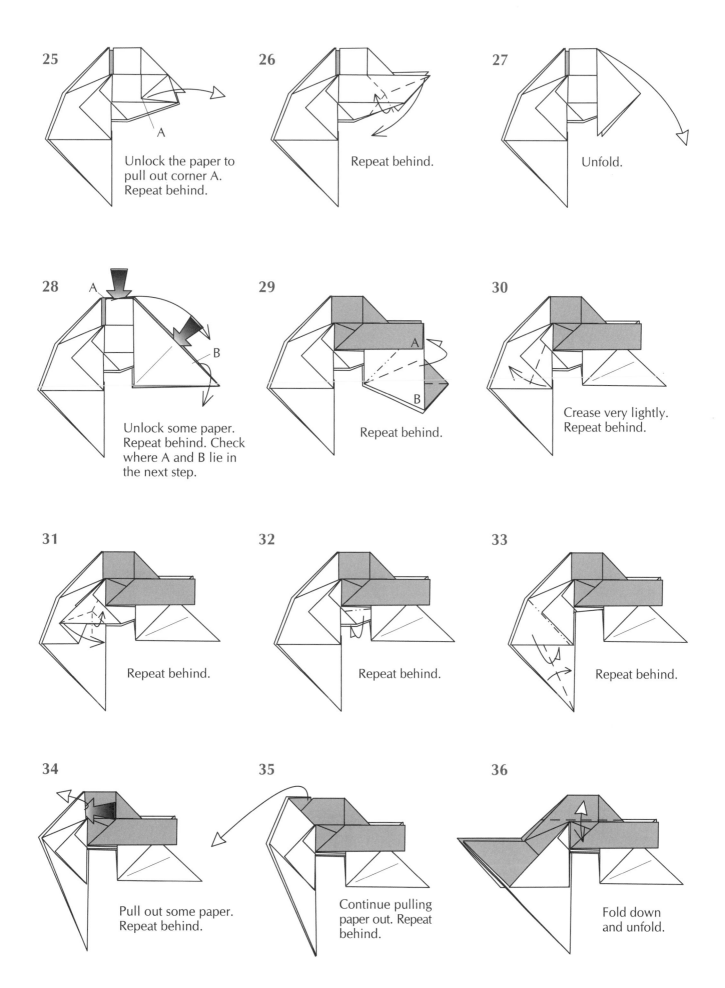

25

Unlock the paper to pull out corner A. Repeat behind.

26

Repeat behind.

27

Unfold.

28

Unlock some paper. Repeat behind. Check where A and B lie in the next step.

29

Repeat behind.

30

Crease very lightly. Repeat behind.

31

Repeat behind.

32

Repeat behind.

33

Repeat behind.

34

Pull out some paper. Repeat behind.

35

Continue pulling paper out. Repeat behind.

36

Fold down and unfold.

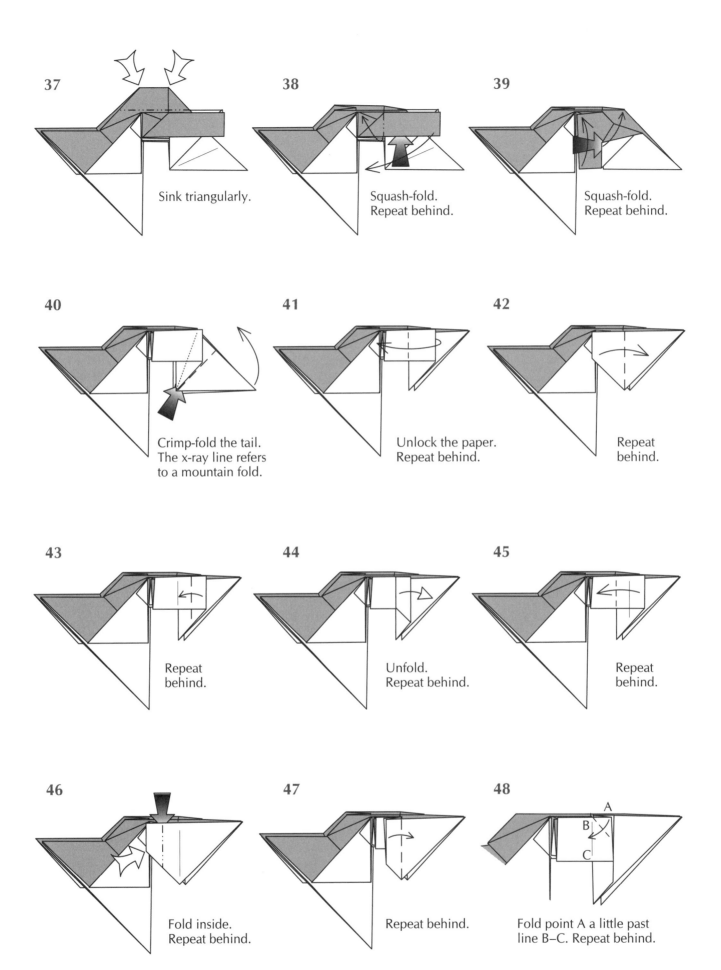

37

Sink triangularly.

38

Squash-fold.
Repeat behind.

39

Squash-fold.
Repeat behind.

40

Crimp-fold the tail.
The x-ray line refers
to a mountain fold.

41

Unlock the paper.
Repeat behind.

42

Repeat
behind.

43

Repeat
behind.

44

Unfold.
Repeat behind.

45

Repeat
behind.

46

Fold inside.
Repeat behind.

47

Repeat behind.

48

A

B

C

Fold point A a little past
line B–C. Repeat behind.

49

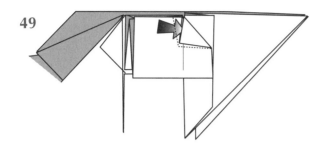

Spread apart to the dotted
lines to form a thin, triangular
stripe. Repeat behind.

50

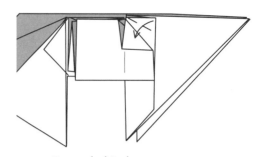

Repeat behind.

51

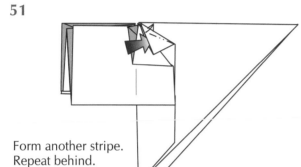

Form another stripe.
Repeat behind.

52

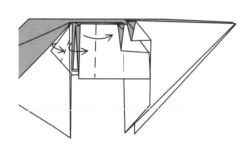

Fold all these layers. Stagger
them to form three more
stripes. Repeat behind.

53

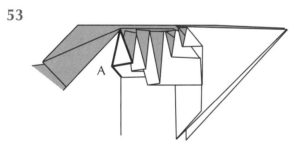

Tuck the left side of the
bold triangle under region
A. Repeat behind.

54

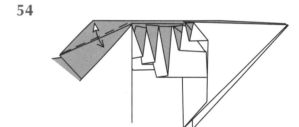

Fold down and unfold.
Repeat behind.

55

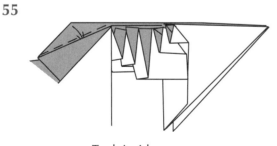

Tuck inside.
Repeat behind.

56

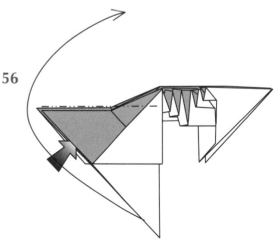

Reverse-fold up.

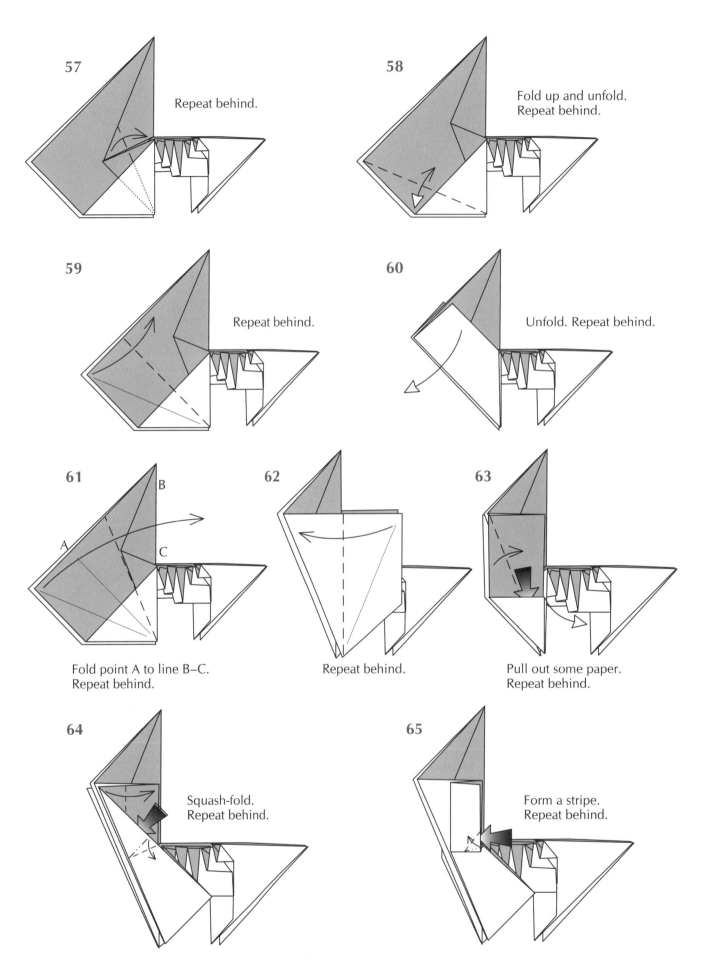

57 Repeat behind.

58 Fold up and unfold. Repeat behind.

59 Repeat behind.

60 Unfold. Repeat behind.

61 Fold point A to line B–C. Repeat behind.

62 Repeat behind.

63 Pull out some paper. Repeat behind.

64 Squash-fold. Repeat behind.

65 Form a stripe. Repeat behind.

66

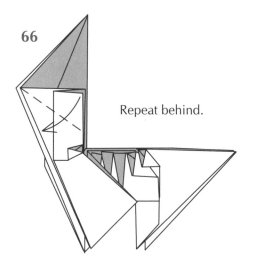

Repeat behind.

67

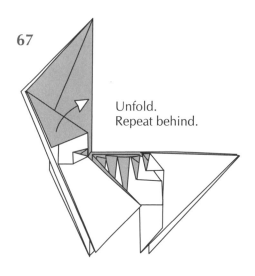

Unfold.
Repeat behind.

68

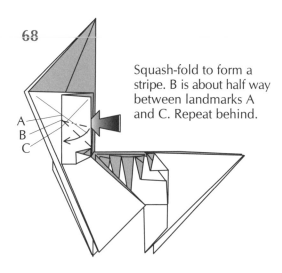

Squash-fold to form a
stripe. B is about half way
between landmarks A
and C. Repeat behind.

A
B
C

69

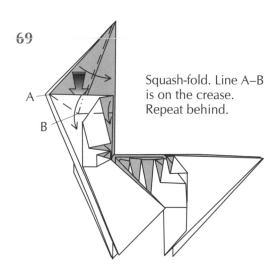

Squash-fold. Line A–B
is on the crease.
Repeat behind.

A
B

70

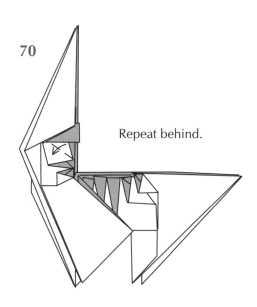

Repeat behind.

71

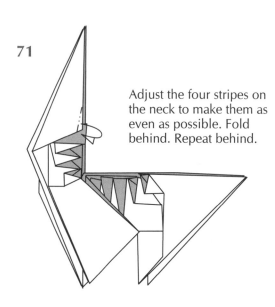

Adjust the four stripes on
the neck to make them as
even as possible. Fold
behind. Repeat behind.

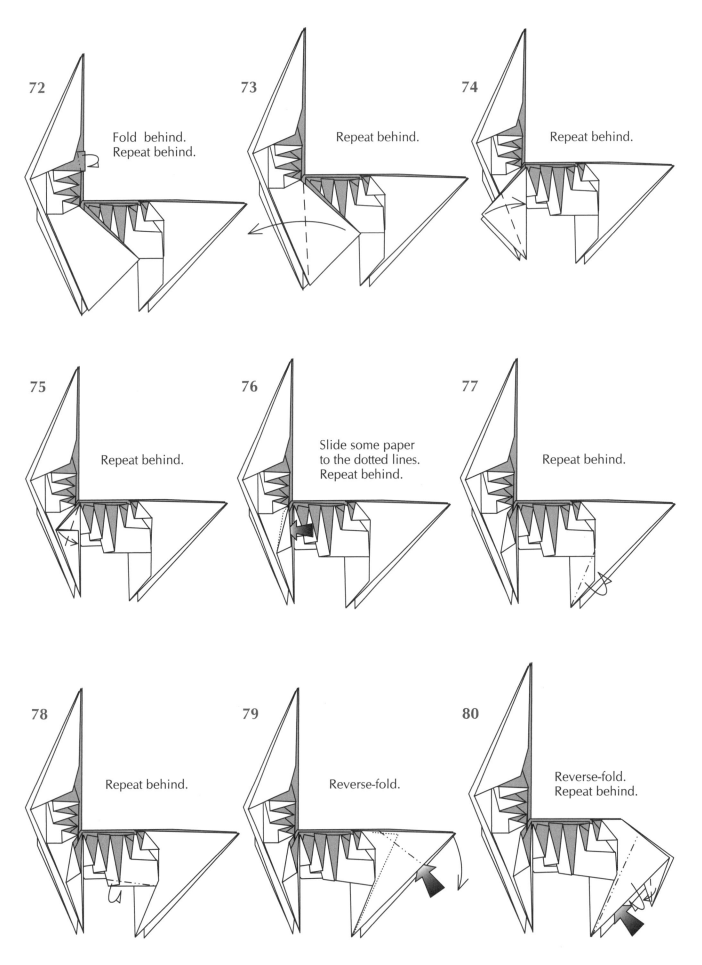

72

Fold behind.
Repeat behind.

73

Repeat behind.

74

Repeat behind.

75

Repeat behind.

76

Slide some paper
to the dotted lines.
Repeat behind.

77

Repeat behind.

78

Repeat behind.

79

Reverse-fold.

80

Reverse-fold.
Repeat behind.

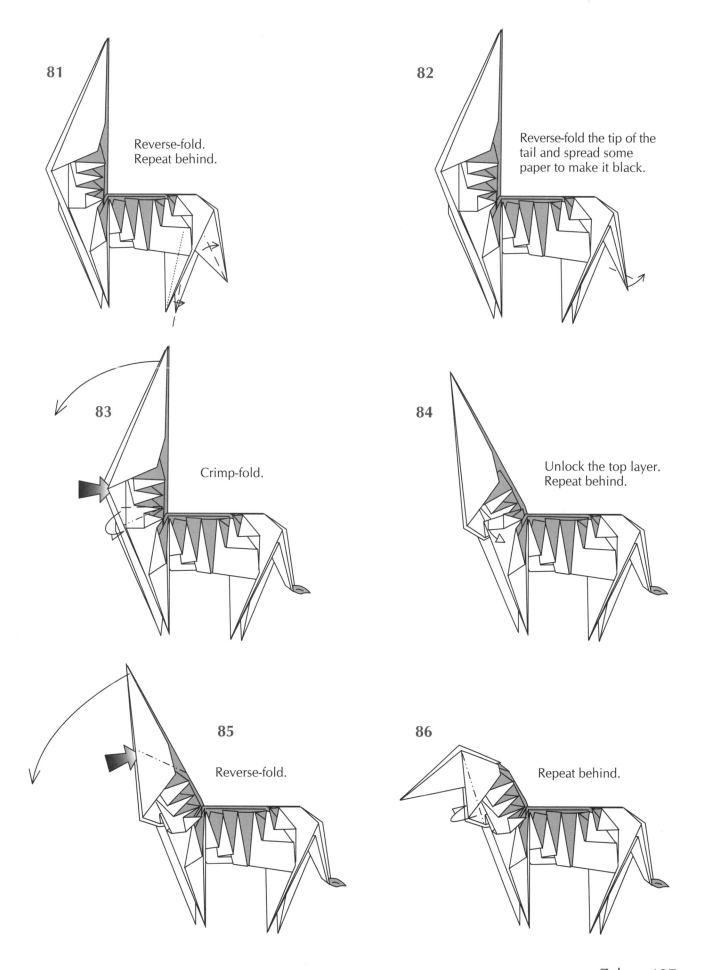

81 Reverse-fold. Repeat behind.

82 Reverse-fold the tip of the tail and spread some paper to make it black.

83 Crimp-fold.

84 Unlock the top layer. Repeat behind.

85 Reverse-fold.

86 Repeat behind.

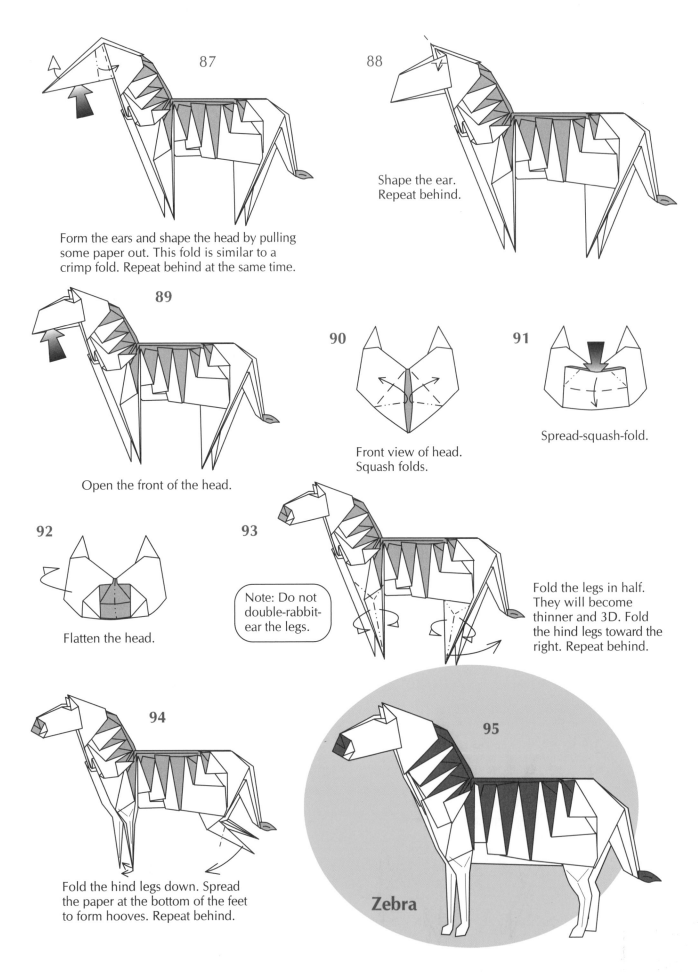

87

Form the ears and shape the head by pulling some paper out. This fold is similar to a crimp fold. Repeat behind at the same time.

88

Shape the ear. Repeat behind.

89

Open the front of the head.

90

Front view of head. Squash folds.

91

Spread-squash-fold.

92

Flatten the head.

93

Note: Do not double-rabbit-ear the legs.

Fold the legs in half. They will become thinner and 3D. Fold the hind legs toward the right. Repeat behind.

94

Fold the hind legs down. Spread the paper at the bottom of the feet to form hooves. Repeat behind.

95

Zebra